LEARN TO RAPID-READ

Ben E. Johnson

Trinity College

HOWARD W. SAMS & CO., INC.

INDIANAPOLIS · KANSAS CITY · NEW YORK

Preface

THE SKILLS OF rapid reading which you will be exposed to in this book can be learned in a relatively short time and without any loss of reading comprehension. They are a summary of the same skills taught in the remarkably successful Achieving Greater Potential (AGP) Rapid-Reading seminars. This unique course began with a college professor who wanted to develop an educationally sound course in rapid reading. He has succeeded. In the past three years, thousands of participants have tested the program in schools, colleges, businesses, and public sessions and have had outstanding results. A constant computerized evaluation of these results reveals that most participants have tripled their normal reading and study speeds.

A grasp of the reading principles in this book accomplishes five things for most participants: (1) it accelerates reading speed; (2) it teaches reading flexibility; (3) it builds word grouping ability; (4) it introduces the concept of pacing; (5) it builds comprehension of material read. For both the average and above-average reader, learning these five things enables them to overcome inefficient reading habits that have accumulated over the years. This growth is accomplished by stressing the underlying principles of reading improvement while adding recent developmental reading innovations, and not by using expensive reading machines.

This book does not teach nor seek "super speeds" that have been achieved by a few experienced rapid readers, but, remember, you, like everyone else, can expect to at least triple your beginning reading rate if you practice the techniques taught in this book.

It requires no magic to improve your reading skills under the AGP instruction in this book, but it will demand practice and persistence if you would like to develop your skills to their full capacity.

The format of the following material enables you to move from one reading skill to the next at your own leisure and as you increase your ability. This will keep you from being unduly pressured or bound to a classroom where other participants may tend to limit your progress. However, we do encourage you to share this book with others. Perhaps the members of your family, your friends at work, or even members of your school class could study the techniques and practice the exercises together, thus enabling you to share a very rewarding and growth facilitating experience.

BEN E. JOHNSON

For Steven, Susan, and Shelley

Contents

Preliminaries

The increasing demands on our time by a variety of school, vocational, avocational, family, and community responsibilities often leave us very little time to devote to the reading of the many books and periodicals that are essential if we are to keep abreast of what is important to us. Often it is difficult for us to keep up with the daily newspaper (A typical Sunday issue of any major newspaper averages 300,000 to 400,000 words, or the equivalent of three or four full-length novels. Try and read all that on one day!), and we certainly know how difficult it often is to find time each day for that personal and private reading which we do purely for pleasure. This book is an attempt to give the busy person, whether he be skilled tradesman, school teacher, student, office worker, executive, civil servant, administrator, or simply the actively reading individual, an overview of reading problems common to most readers, an understanding of how these problems can be overcome, and an insight into how more efficient reading habits can be particularly helpful in the reading you are required to do every day on the job, all that reading for school, or even the reading you do for pleasure. Are you interested in any of these areas? Certainly. And you have been for years. Let's get started.

How Fast Do You Read Now?

As you may expect, it is necessary at the outset to discover your present reading rate, and that will be done in two ways. The first is a standardized test of reading comprehension (The *Bendic Test of Reading Comprehension,* Form A) which follows. Read the instructions and then time yourself for four minutes, or, better yet, have someone else time you as you take the test. Then, using the answer key at the end of the test, score your test and determine your comprehension score. A similar test of the same level of difficulty (Form B) is at the end of this book and will enable you to determine to what extent your comprehension has increased.

Bendic Test of Reading Comprehension
Form A
Directions

1. A number of selected sentences are printed. Each sentence is printed as the sentence below:
   Ideally, promotion policy should allow each child to be ~~results~~ with the group in which he can make the best total adjustment, socially and educationally.

2. You are to read the sentence. In so doing you will note that an absurd word has been inserted. This inserted word has no relation to the meaning of the rest of the sentence.

3. You are to draw a line through the absurd word. In the sentence above, the absurd word is "results." Draw the line through the word "results." Do it.

4. On the following pages read each sentence as you come to it. As soon as you have found the absurd word, cross it out and go on to the next sentence. Do not skip about. This is primarily a test of your comprehension but it is also a test of your rate of reading; therefore work rapidly but carefully.

5. Now, allow exactly four minutes to take the test and then score your own test. Your reading rate for four minutes has already been figured. It is the score in the left margin.

9.7   1. The ~~absence~~ former book called essentially for a broad interpretation of an entire period and of material already known, and permitted the discussion of particular or new aspects only in so far as they illustrated larger points of view.

17.5   2. Your desire of visiting Europe is very natural, and is dictated by views so honorable that ~~intelligent~~ I hope you will find some real occasion by which it may be gratified.

22.5   3. The world has already been amazingly complex, and with our widening understanding comes a sometimes paralyzing awareness of ~~dissatisfied its~~ complexity.

33.4 4. It was a picture of a boss who had to have ~~his~~ his own way no matter what, a picture business of a boss that nobody could talk to, a picture of a boss who humiliated his staff with petty regulations and unwanted favors.

42 5. For example, it is better to be eternal than ~~satire~~ not to be eternal, to be good than not to be good, indeed, to be goodness itself rather than not to be goodness itself.

49.5 6. However, by the end of the first or sometime during the second grade, the early advantage in lose word recognition produces better vocabulary and comprehension scores on silent reading tests.

57.4 7. Members of mature groups find in them the means for meeting their basic needs and ~~transferred~~ their effect, generally, is to reduce the anxieties to their numbers rather than to raise them.

62.1 8. So my Lord did give order for weighing anchor, ~~permanent~~ which we did, and sailed all day.

65.8 9. The sacrifice established a merit ~~advise~~ before God designed to induce His blessing upon the offerer.

71.3 10. This feeling of commonality can often be elicited by your suggesting that your own beliefs are commonly held by ~~amount~~ others.

78.8 11. In the seventeenth century the use of coal, the technique of experimentation in applied science, and the application of capital to industrial development had inaugurated what has been called ~~article~~ The Industrial Revolution.

86.2 12. Yes, to me also was ~~appear~~ given, if not victory, yet the consciousness of battle, and the resolve to persevere therein while life or faculty is left.

97.1 13. Whoever ~~efficiency~~ would see the American people as remarkable for their philosophy as they are for their industry, enterprise, and political freedom must be gratified that these works have already attracted considerable attention among us and are beginning to exert no little influence on our philosophical speculations.

102.5   14. No prophecy ever came by the impulse of man, but men moved by the Holy Spirit spoke from oppose God.

114   15. Following the war between the states teaching became a woman's profession to an extent not true in any other great nation in the world; however, following World War I and World controversy War II, more women are teaching in other great nations than ever before.

117   16. Thus it was emphasized that the fight against Moscow was first on Peking's order believe of priority.

121   17. He was alone, however, and the determined stand of significance France was supported by the three Eastern powers.

128.1   18. In a literal sense, therefore, the new instrument grew out of the political life of Americans time themselves in the colonial and revolutionary periods.

135   19. It is, after all, extremely difficult to separate (even for purposes of analysis) the influence of the law itself from that of the social disapproval inevitably accompanying occurring it.

140.1   20. At the moment it still seems to be the best way, at least until we develop an agricultural technology for except dealing with lateritic soils.

147.1   21. Suppose I try to allotment see each of these debtors as people who are faced with serious problems that are getting them into debt.

151.3   22. In any case, military preparations did not guarantee success subtle against invaders, and compulsory service was not even considered by them.

155.3   23. I would not agree with them to prove my condescension, nor differ from them to forty mark my independence.

161.8   24. Still other research relevant principle to beginning reading had been carried on in the clinic in the form of case studies.

166.6   25. Performing before an hypocritic audience I would think about how great I was, and had no special interest in the people of the audience.

179.1   26. In instrumental surprise music we could mention many virtuosi among the Germans and thereby prove, supposing that were our intention, that they are to be preferred even to the most celebrated Italians as virtuosi on various instruments and at the same time as composers.

188   27. While looking round his shop for the particular bonbons or jujubes I wanted, he would lend an ear to the conversation kept up by his tall wife and lean consistent daughters in the next room.

196.8   28. But much of the anxiety of the leader or supervisor is the perceive result of the attitudes and feelings about authority which he developed toward authority when he was a person of lesser importance—yes, even when he was a child.

200.8   29. Knowledge of these affairs disappoint derives from letters which passed among various officials containing orders, reports, and complaints.

209.8   30. The morning sun was still low in the sky; it was cold and possession cheerless, casting long shadows over the thinly snow-crusted ground.

215.5   31. The man's skin was wrinkled and weathered, and he coughed in occasional rapid spurts, shooting characterize out little puggs of steam, like a starting locomotive with skidding wheels.

229.8   32. Some notion may be formed of its exaltation and glory by attentively considering the sensible world in its greatness, its beauty, and the order of its ceaseless motion, and then by rising to the contemplation of its avenger archetype in the pure and changeless being of the intelligible world, and then by recognizing in intelligence the author and finisher of all.

236.6   33. Stimuli can then be applied to the area served by that nerve trunk and the advise discharge of the single fiber can be studied.

240.6   34. The varies jug had evidently been once filled with water, as it was covered inside with green mold.

246.3   35. No one protects the rights of fisherman, swimmers, or just the poor benighted souls who don't led like the stink and slime.

252.1   36. Some phosphate bonds are very rich in energy, and compounds that separation include such bonds are utilized in metabolism a great deal.

257.8   37. As you have seen, I definition attempt to convert the names into symbols of images which are then concrete and clearly recallable.

263.3   38. I have taken you through this formula step-description by-step to show you the basic format for remembering a financial statement.

269.5   39. We say that the king can do no wrong; different we say that to do wrong is the property not of power, but of weakness.

276.3   40. I get him to smoke hopeless the pipe for a couple of weeks, then put in a new stem, and continue operations as long as the pipe holds together.

282.1   41. When and what type of variations arise in possible a population or become lost by genetic drift is mainly a matter of chance.

288.5   42. This does not necessarily mean that the equations original describe the biological system; the equations may be related to the biological system only in the abstract.

294.8   43. One good turn deserved another and bury the correspondent hoped to gain from a shepherd a promised goat in return.

298   44. They cigarettes have a chance to make it if we can give them some food to tide them over.

305   45. In financier one respect the emperor's views of his position and policy had now verred around into full accord with the desires of Spain.

308.6   46. He is able to protect, deliver, rescue, and save, help, liberate and redeem scene his devotees.

312.6   47. He had assumed the heavy task of giving a mathematical demonstration of the spirituality of the soul fundamental.

320.3   48. Now, since the incorporation of Navarre with Castile, they had acquired a vital interest in the struggle with France plausible which would be necessary to retain it.

324   49. Often such an attractive margin fantasy intoxicates the suicidal mind, and tips the scale to death.

329.1   50. Now a stone exists, an animal lives; but I accusers don't think a stone lives or an animal understands.

Answer Key to Form A

The extra word is:

1. absence	18. time	35. led
2. intelligent	19. occurring	36. separation
3. dissatisfied	20. except	37. definition
4. business	21. allotment	38. description
5. satire	22. subtle	39. different
6. lose	23. forty	40. hopeless
7. transferred	24. principle	41. possible
8. permanent	25. hypocrite	42. original
9. advise	26. surprise	43. bury
10. amount	27. consistent	44. cigarettes
11. article	28. perceive	45. financier
12. appear	29. disappoint	46. scene
13. efficiency	30. possession	47. fundamental
14. oppose	31. characterize	48. plausible
15. controversy	32. avenger	49. margin
16. believe	33. advise	50. accusers
17. significance	34. varies	

The second way to discover your present reading speed in relatively light reading is to read for five minutes in a novel of your choice. (Before you go any further, get a novel. Right now. You will be using this novel often as you continue through this book, so keep it handy.) Have someone time you now as you read for five minutes. Read as you normally do, and with good comprehension. When your five minutes are up, figure your reading rate. Here's how: Simply figure the average number of words per line by counting the words in three lines and then dividing by 3. The answer is the average number of words per line for your novel. Count the total number of lines read in five minutes, multiply the number of lines read by the average number of words per line in your book. Your answer is the total number of words read in five minutes. Now divide that total by 5 (minutes read). The quotient is your words-per-minute rate for the novel.

Record Your Scores

To discover how fast you are progressing in the learning of new reading skills, use the Progress Chart on page 176. Record on this chart each reading rate as you determine it, including the scores for the two timed tests that you have just completed. The bottom vertical lines allow you to identify the selection read and the length of time spent reading. The vertical middle lines show the number of words per minute that were read. Put a dot at the height corresponding to your reading rate and enter it on the vertical line corresponding to each selection. Connect the dots for each selection by a straight line, so you can view your progress in graph form.

Did you have a higher rate of reading with the novel? Probably, because it was easier reading than the test. *A significant factor to remember in reading rate is that everything you read has different levels of difficulty and thus will be read at different speeds.*

For general reading, however, a rate of 175-250 words per minute is about average.

1

Fundamentals of Rapid Reading

You Are Now Ready to Begin

The next several pages will answer these basic questions:

1. What is rapid reading?
2. On what kinds of reading do rapid reading techniques prove useful?
3. What maximum speed can I reach?
4. What prevents one from reading rapidly?
5. Upon what principles are the techniques of rapid reading based, and how does understanding these principles allow for instant increase of reading speed?
6. Why does pacing play such a large part in rapid reading?
7. What is the importance of eye-hand coordination?

For the next few minutes ponder these questions and try to answer them in your mind. Then, as you read the following pages, find out if you came close to the right answers.

Typical Kinds of Readers and Reading Problems

There are three kinds of readers. You fit into one of the following categories. Identify the kind of reader you are.

1. *The Motor Reader*—reads around 150 words per minute in general reading.
2. *The Auditory Reader*—reads around 300 words per minute.
3. *The Visual Reader*—reads 800 + words per minute.

The reason that the *motor reader,* often called a "vocalizer," is limited to about 150 wpm is that this is the approximate speed at which he talks. Since he uses his tongue, lips, or organs of speech to form the words he is silently reading, he is restricted to this relatively low level of reading because it is as fast as he can mouth the words. In addition, he occasionally disturbs those around him by whispering when he reads, and he tires easily because he works so hard at reading. The motor reader is still reading aloud (although he may have his mouth closed) as he was taught to read in the elementary grades. All of us have some tendency to vocalize as we read, but these problems can be overcome with effort and concentration on improved reading techniques which you are about to learn.

The *auditory reader* imagines each word of print, often unnecessarily visualizing the words in great detail as he reads them. He is a word *thinker* and a word *hearer,* often concentrating so intently on each word that he can hear it pronounced as it is silently read. For example, when the auditory reader sees the word "tree" he may see a specific tree, perhaps a cherry tree, and even see cherries on the branches. Obviously this degree of visual detail is unnecessary.

The *visual reader* passes the words directly to the comprehension without any stops in between. He reads rapidly but efficiently and allows no wasted effort. To be a visual reader is the goal of every reader. Nothing should be said, nothing heard, everything *seen.*

Now that you are persuaded that you would like to be a visual reader, let's get to the "secret" of rapid reading so that you can move your eyes in a flashing blur across each line, right? Wrong. You need to understand something else first.

What Hinders Rapid Reading?

When you ask the average person what keeps him from reading as rapidly as he would wish to read, he is likely to mention a variety of barriers: distractions, hot room, poor vocabulary, drowsiness, lack of interest (or too much interest) and many other things. But no matter what things are mentioned there are two major problems that he probably will not mention and they are the most important hindrances to rapid reading: regression and fixation.

Regression is the reversion of the eyes to words read previously. This is normally a subconscious desire on the part of the reader to check up on himself—to reassure himself that what he saw was really there. This occurs especially with long words or unfamiliar words and concepts.

It is difficult to avoid the conclusion that smaller schools will find it necessary to rethink their roles as the task of providing funds for adequate operation becomes more formidable. Already there is a growing conviction that modern education must lay aside the once hallowed idea of the value of small institutions and accept the notion that quality professional education demands a sizeable heterogeneous community. It is thus no longer so simple to validate expensive small operations on the basis of higher quality.

Since this regression is usually an unconscious occurrence it is difficult to correct unless the eye is simply forced to move forward consistently. In inefficient readers, regression may occur 50% or more of the time spent reading. This means that for every ten words the eyes move forward they move backward five words! You can see that this will certainly slow down a reader! Even in relatively efficient readers, regression occurs up to 25% of the time.

Fixation—the stopping of the eyes on a word—is a natural and necessary thing in that the eye must stop (fixate) to record symbols on the brain. If the eyes were continually moving they could not focus and thus could not perceive. The problems come in *stopping too long* on a word or group of words, or in *stopping too often* on a line. The eyes of an average reader are physically capable of perceiving at speeds up to ⅟₁₀₀ of a second. However, most readers take four times that long on each fixation. One major reason for this unnecessary slowness dates back to those familiar words of our elementary school days: "Slow down and sound it out." Remember? Each time we came to a new word or an unfamiliar word, we were told to slow down and proceed cautiously. We may not be proceeding cautiously any more, but we have certainly slowed down from the rapidity with which we could habitually move our eyes. If you will train your eyes to stop in briefer fixations, you will find an amazing increase in your reading speed. To move from ⅟₂₅ of a second per fixation to ⅟₅₀ of a second will result in a doubling of your reading rate and is quite within the realm of each person's possibility. More about this later in the book.

Stopping too often is also a fixation problem. With training, our eyes are capable of seeing, at each fixation, twice as many letters as we now see. The average reader takes in five to six letters at a fixation when he is reading. With steady effort he can increase what he sees to ten to twelve letters per fixation. The following illustrations show the average person's fixations and then show the fixation patterns of an efficient reader on the same paragraph.

Average Reader

Mrs. Miller was in the inner room with her daughter, whence

the maid presently brought a message to Mr. Jones that her

mistress hoped he would excuse the disappointment, but

an accident had happened which made it impossible for her

to have the pleasure of his company at breakfast that day;

and begged his pardon for not sending him up notice sooner.

Efficient Reader

Mrs. Miller was in the inner room with her daughter, whence

the maid presently brought a message to Mr. Jones that her

mistress hoped he would excuse the disappointment, but an

accident had happened which made it impossible for her

to have the pleasure of his company at breakfast that day;

and begged his pardon for not sending him up notice sooner.

You can see that doubling the span of perception, by itself, would double a person's reading rate, and with normal if not increased comprehension. Again, more will be said about this later in the book.

Overcoming Regression and Fixation Problems

If regression and fixation are the two major problems in increasing our habitual reading rate, the question obviously becomes one of what to do to overcome these problems. A beginning answer involves the concept of pacing.

What Is Pacing?

Pacing is defined as "forcing, by some method, the eyes to move in a directed pattern across the lines and down the page." Sometimes expensive reading machines are employed as pacers. Since you do not have access to mechanical pacing devices, you will be taught an efficient pacing method which utilizes the reader's hand as the pacer.

What Difference Does Pacing Make?

Try a pacing experiment. Read for five minutes in the same novel you used earlier. This time, however, pace yourself *with your hand* by using the *Basic-Z* pacing technique illustrated below. This is done by sliding your index finger *under each line as you read.* Let your finger move *slightly ahead of your eyes* as you read, thus in effect pulling your eyes along each line.

Be sure not to let your finger stop on a word. Keep moving and keep your finger only *slightly* ahead of your eyes.

Remember: It is important that you comprehend what you read, so don't go too fast. If you are concentrating on your hand, but forgetting what you read, slow down.

In summary:
1. Keep moving.
2. Only slightly ahead of your eyes.
3. Read for normal comprehension.

Basic-Z Pattern

Your hand and your eyes should follow the basic reading pattern on each line as shown in **Fig. 1-1**. After reading for

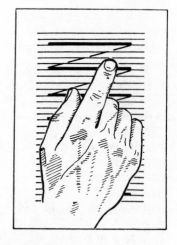

Fig. 1-1. Basic-Z pattern.

five minutes, figure your reading speed and estimate your comprehension. Record your speed and comprehension on your record sheet.

Begin reading now for five minutes.

How Did You Do?

When the Basic-Z pattern is first used, it usually brings an increase in reading speed. Did it for you? The reason for this increase is quite simple: the eyes have a tendency to follow motion. As the pacing finger moves across the line, the eyes follow it, thereby cutting down the habitual regression pattern of the reader and establishing a rhythmic movement of the eyes so that fixations are not of unnecessarily long duration. You may want to try two or three five-minute readings until you begin to pace with a little less rigidity and a little less self-consciousness.

What Is Reading Flexibility?

Your speed will vary according to the difficulty of the material you are reading. As you read more difficult material you will find that your speed suffers, but you ought to expect this. *Different kinds of materials ought to be read at different speeds.* For instance, you may read a novel at 250 wpm and a logic book at 125 wpm. But if you double your reading rate in one, you will probably also double in the other. The novel will then be read at 500 wpm and the logic book will be read at 250 wpm. These techniques can still be utilized no matter how difficult the material, and you ought to attempt to be as flexible as possible in applying your new skills to all types of reading. With increased practice comes increased efficiency.

Nearly all reading machines, such as the tachistoscope and reading accelerator, operate on the same principle of pacing. The eyes are forced by some method (a moving T-bar, a beam of light, a shutter) to keep moving along the line and down the page. The obvious advantage of using your finger as a pacer is that you always have it with you and you can use it on all types of reading materials. Since reading efficiency depends on practice, you are not limited to a classroom. You can practice efficient reading every time you read.

As you continue Basic-Z practice for the next few days, concentrate on developing eye-hand coordination. You will experience successful rapid reading as you develop a smoothness and rhythm in leading your eyes across the lines and down the page.

Practice Tips

In your practice, be sure to do the following:

1. Be sure that you are comfortable at your desk or table.
2. Place the hand with which you are planning to pace (pacing hand) on the page to be read, and with your index finger extended, point slightly ahead of the place at which you intend to begin reading.
3. Begin slowly, gliding your index finger along each line, reading just behind it, increasing your speed of movement as you are able.

NOTE: At this point be sure that you don't sacrifice comprehension for speed. Do not proceed any further in this book until you have practiced Basic-Z pacing for several days and find that you can pace from habit without consciously thinking about moving your hand. When pacing becomes a habit for you, you will find that your comprehension of what you read is also increased. Your reading progress will be much better if you read at normal comprehension, never allowing yourself to read so rapidly that you miss what you read! Both speed and comprehension will increase if you are conscious of *both* as you read. Above all, do not neglect to *practice* at least 30 minutes a day. Use the reading techniques you are learning. This will allow for better gains and is the only way to ensure permanent improvement. As with all skills, confidence and success in rapid reading will come with continued use. So use the pacing techniques you learn on all kinds of reading . . . both pleasure and technical.

2

Four Acceleration Techniques

Now that you've mastered the concept of Basic-Z pacing you are ready for the further acceleration techniques presented in the following pages. These techniques will give you an immediate increase of 10% or more in your reading rate the first time you try them.

1. Reading indentation
2. Rapid return
3. Book holding
4. Page turning

Remember, like everything else in this book, to master the four techniques that can help accelerate your reading, practice is essential. Begin by practicing the first of the four techniques: indentation.

Indentation

Take any reading material that you have handy—your novel will do fine—and draw straight lines down through the print approximately one-half inch in from each margin as shown in Fig. 2-1.

The purpose of these lines is to provide limits for your eyes and for your pacing finger. You are to look at only the words between the lines. As you read you will notice that you see the words on the outsides of the lines, although you are not looking beyond the vertical lines you have drawn. Your eyes will still see the words on the other sides of the lines, but you will save reading time by not looking directly

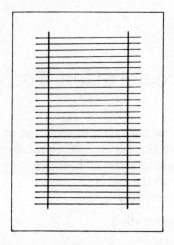

Fig. 2-1. Indention for reading.

at those words. In fact, by indenting one-half inch at each edge you will be able to save at least 25% of your reading time because the printed lines you are reading are now only about three-fourths as long. Practice reading with indentation for several pages. Then try reading several pages without drawing the lines but still not permitting yourself to read within one-half inch of each margin. Do you see how it gets increasingly easy to stay within the lines while still seeing the whole line? Practice until you've begun to establish this new habit of indentation.

Rapid Return

As your eyes return to the beginning of each new line, they may move as rapidly as forty-thousandths of a second. It is important that the rapid return of the eyes is not jerky or hesitating, but even and rhythmical, so that speed is at an optimum. The next exercise will help your eyes to return rapidly, efficiently, and smoothly to each new line.

Begin practicing rapid return on the next illustration. Practice swinging your eyes from block to block. Go over this exercise on Fig. 2-2 at least ten times before turning the page.

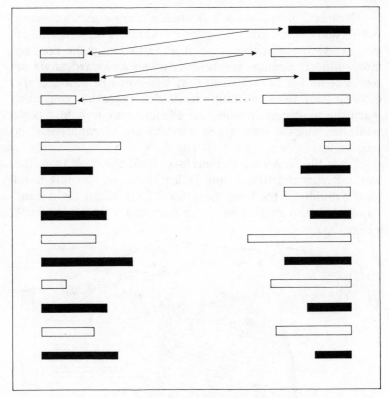

Fig. 2-2. Rapid return.

Now you are ready to practice your rapid-return sweep in your novel. Turn to any page and for three to five minutes try to develop an efficient return sweep by reading just the beginning and ending of the lines. It is not essential to get full comprehension, but if you see the full line, that's fine. Don't forget to use your Basic-Z pacing technique as you practice your rapid return. Begin reading, and practice until your return seems effortless.

Book Holding

You will be surprised at the simplicity of the third acceleration technique which will make an astounding difference in your reading: Hold the book properly.

Because holding a book is such a simple matter, many people don't think about it, they merely hold on with one or two hands or sometimes none at all. This can make reading more difficult because the book is at an awkward angle or too close or too far away so that the eyes are strained. To develop your reading ability to its full potential, you must learn the most comfortable and efficient way to hold a book while reading—a way which permits use of rapid reading techniques.

Place the book on a flat surface. Hold the book from the top and rest the thumb and index finger of the left hand on the middle of the book margins and top of the right hand page while the remaining three fingers are under the book (Fig. 2-3).

Fig. 2-3. Holding the book.

This allows for easily holding the book open. It also keeps the book inclined slightly at a comfortable angle of vision. The print at the top of the page should be the same distance from your eyes as the print at the bottom of the page. A good distance to hold the book from the eyes is approximately 14 inches or about the distance from your shoulder to your elbow. Speed and comprehension increase when you are relaxed with little or no eyestrain.

Page Turning

You can now add a great time-saver to your reading skill if you are holding your book properly. It is very simple. You merely use your left index finger to turn the pages while you are holding on to the top of the book with the same hand. As you are reading the right-hand page, you insert your left index finger under the top right-hand corner of the page so that when you finish reading the page you can flip it from the top without stopping the pacing pattern with your right hand. Immediately begin reading the left-hand page. Your left index finger should automatically insert itself under the new right-hand page (Fig. 2-4). Turning pages this way will avoid the usual fumbling to turn the pages as we finish reading, and will enable us to maintain the pacing rhythm.

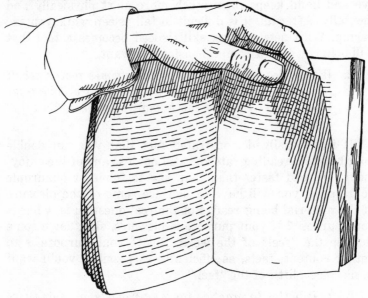

Fig. 2-4. Turning the page.

For the next thirty to forty pages in your novel, practice turning pages until this new technique becomes natural to you. Once you begin using this technique on a regular basis you will find that your reading efficiency and ease are increased.

Common Questions About Speed in Reading

We have been stressing ways to increase your reading speed, so usually about this point in the course you probably have a few questions.

1. *When I increase my reading speed, don't I lose comprehension?*

The fear among beginning rapid reading students that comprehension will drop as speed goes up is quite common. On the contrary, however, most readers find that their comprehension goes up as they increase speed because they are concentrating much more on their reading than they ever did before. Also, they often find that the coordination of eye and hand keeps them much more alert physically and mentally. After all, it is difficult to fall asleep while you are pacing. With new reading skills speed becomes a tool that will help you get the comprehension you want.

2. *When I learn to read two or three times faster, won't I enjoy the mood, the tone, the "feel" of a book less? Won't I lose some of the humor, freshness, "beauty" of a work?*

It is an easily demonstrated fact that you can double your habitual reading rate and still not lose any of the enjoyment. To read faster than that, say to triple or quadruple your speed, you will have to sacrifice some of the pleasure of the material being read. But the real question is, what is your purpose? If your purpose is pleasure, slow down some to keep the "feel" of the work. But if your purpose is to gather content, facts, as efficiently as possible, you'll want to sacrifice a little of the "feel."

3. *Is it better to practice for long periods, once or twice a week, or for brief periods daily?*

Practice for brief periods (30 minutes or so) every day will help you build efficient reading habits faster than if you practice for long periods only occasionally.

4. *If I feel I already know some of what is being taught in this book, can I skip to what seems to be new and more beneficial?*

In a word, no! Do not skip around; proceed step by step through the book. Even if some of the material sounds familiar, do not skip it. Perhaps it only *sounds* familiar. Even if it is familiar, the review will be helpful to you.

3

Four Advanced
Pacing Techniques

The next part of this book introduces four advanced pacing movements and will show you how much pacing increases reading skill and efficiency. These additional pacing movements are called "comfort patterns" because they are designed to provide a comfortable alternative to the Basic Z. While most people find the Basic-Z pattern quite effective, for some people it is limiting, uncomfortable, awkward, too rigid, or has any number of other problems. Reading experts and educational psychologists have known for many years that if a person is uncomfortable, nervous, or tense, his reading speed and comprehension will be severely affected. Just the opposite is true if a person reads while relaxed and comfortable—his reading rate and comprehension are always high. Therefore, as you practice the next four pacing patterns, ask yourself the following questions:

1. How does this pattern feel? Is it easy for me to do? Do I "like" it?

2. Is my reading rate greater with this pattern than with the other patterns I've tried to this point?

3. How is my comprehension? Do I retain as much or more while using this pattern?

Remember, a pacing pattern of some sort is always going to be necessary if you intend to retain a faster reading rate. If you complete this rapid reading instruction and then decide not to use a pacing technique, your built-up reading speed will quickly diminish. While you may not return to the slow speed at which you were before the instruction (obviously you will have learned some reading skills that will be with you forever), without constantly pacing yourself in some way, your eyes will very quickly fall back into their old lazy and inefficient ways of reading.

Your goal now should be to find at least two pacing patterns with which you can feel comfortable as you read. Which two? It doesn't matter. Any two that are comfortable for you.

Wiggle

The following pacing technique is called the "Wiggle." Practice it on the following reading selection. The Wiggle technique involves placing the open hand, palm down, on the page and without excessive motion gently moving the fingers back and forth across the page, guiding your eyes (Fig. 3-1). One of the benefits of this motion is that it is a relaxed and natural pattern which most people find easy to do. It also covers much of the print on the page so that the eyes are hindered in their attempts to glance ahead as they move along the line. Reread the selection if your compre-

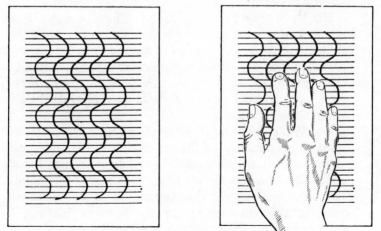

Fig. 3-1. Wiggle technique.

hension is not normal while using the Wiggle. Be sure to record your words-per-minute rate after you read the selection.

How the Men From Mars Ruined a Quiet Evening*
by Ben Gross

It was a pleasant little dinner with a few friends in a Tudor City apartment on a Sunday evening in October, 1938.

"How about turning on Charlie McCarthy?" one of the guests said.

"Okay," I answered, "but do you mind if we first hear what Orson Welles is doing?" Just a few days before, at CBS headquarters, I asked one of the actors of Welles' "Mercury Theatre of the Air" about Sunday's show.

"Just between us," he had said, "it's lousy. Orson couldn't get ready the script he wanted, so he's run in a dramatization of the H. G. Wells' chestnut, *The War of the Worlds.*"

"Oh, that," I said.

"Yeah, good old Sunday-supplement fantasy, but he's dressed it up. Anyway, don't bother to listen. Probably bore you to death."

His words had made me happy. There would not be too many programs worthy of comment on the radio the following Sunday, and instead of having to do an entirely new column of comment for the late editions, I should be able to get by merely with the rewriting of two or three brief paragraphs. It would be a quiet and restful Sabbath evening.

But Welles had staged some of the best experimental dramatic productions on the air during that period, and a sense of duty impelled me to eavesdrop on him for at least a few minutes. Even though he might be merely coasting along during this broadcast, if he displayed some ingenuity in dressing up the familiar fantasy, it might be worth a line or two for the *Three Star.*

---

*From *I Looked And I Listened,* Copyright 1954, 1970, by Ben Gross.

The show began conventionally enough, with the announcer saying quite distinctly that the Columbia Broadcasting System and its affiliated stations were presenting Orson Welles and the "Mercury Theatre of the Air" in *The War of the Worlds* by H. G. Wells. Soon we heard a "news flash" which informed us that a tremendous explosion had taken place on the planet Mars.

Now came a veritable cascade of sensational "bulletins." A meteor had crashed near Grover's Mills, New Jersey. More than a thousand persons had been killed. Finally, an "on-the-spot" remote broadcast from the New Jersey countryside. The meteor was no meteor at all; it was a silver cylinder, a miraculous ship from outer space, and from it were streaming horrendous creatures, the like of which had not been seen on this globe before, men from Mars armed with disintegrating and incinerating death-ray guns. There was no defense against these; thousands who had rushed to the field where the craft had landed were being burned to cinders. The Martians had invaded the earth to exterminate its inhabitants!

We had not yet heard of flying saucers, artificial satellites, and other such phenomena; but what came over the air was overwhelmingly terrifying. And the staccato "news reports" and pronouncements by "officials" which followed made it seem even more so. For the National Guard had been called out . . . the Secretary of War was issuing orders to the Army . . . a state of national emergency had been proclaimed . . . the State Department and even the White House were urging the people to keep calm. But what did these appeals matter? By now the Martians were marching on New York!

"You know," I remarked, arising from a half-consumed steak, "I think I'd better be getting back to the office. Some listeners might really believe this."

"How could they?" asked one of the guests. "They announced it was by H. G. Wells. That means it's fiction."

"But those who tuned in late didn't hear the announcement," another said.

It was lucky for me that I had returned to the nearby office. Passing through the city room an assistant at the city desk yelled, "Hey! What the hell's going on?"

The switchboard was blazing; lines were jammed and phones rang all over the place. Rewrite men in booths tried desperately to reach CBS, but none of their calls got through; photographers with full equipment scurried toward the elevators.

"No, madam . . . no, sir . . . we don't know anything about an explosion in Jersey," the man at the switchboard was saying. "Man from Mars?" . . . Yeah, I know it's on the radio . . . but it didn't happen . . . Nothing's going on, I tell you . . . No, madam . . . no, sir . . . there ain't no men from Mars."

A police official's call reached the city desk. "It's just a phony, a radio play," the harassed assistant told him. Then, shouting at me: "You try to get CBS. If you can't, go up there."

The two phones in the radio room were clanging wildly and I grabbed both receivers. "Are they abandoning New York?" a hysterical woman asked over one.

"No, lady, it's just a play," I said.

"Oh, no!" she screamed and hung up.

A Red Cross man was on the other wire.

"I hear they're broadcasting about a terrible catastrophe in New Jersey," said he. "Do you know where?"

It's only Orson Welles," I explained. He's on with a fantasy."

"But my wife just called me and said thousands have been killed," he said.

My assistant rushed in breathless with proofs from the composing room. The phones again. "My God! Those calls have been driving me crazy!" she said.

I made for the door. "You're not going to leave me all alone with these phones?" the distraught girl pleaded. I gave her no heed.

Downstairs, in the cab, the radio was tuned to WEAF. "Get WABC" (the CBS station), I said. The cabbie did, and we heard the calm voice of an announcer saying that this was merely an Orson Welles presentation of a story by H. G. Wells. A few seconds later the Martians were marching again. They had just destroyed Trenton and were, in fact, already on the Palisades, rushing with fiery death on to our metropolis ...

Refugees were scurrying from the city in wild flight ... but that wasn't all ... some of the invaders, who had followed in other ships from outer space, had detoured to the Midwest and the South.

"God Almighty!" the cab driver exclaimed.

"It's just fiction," I assured him. "Didn't you hear the announcer?"

"No, I didn't hear no announcer," the chauffeur said. "You're sure?"

"You don't see any panic-stricken people running about the streets, do you?" I asked.

But just at that moment we passed a movie theatre on Third Avenue. A half-dozen women and children scurried from it as from nearby bars men dashed out to gaze at the sky. On Lexington Avenue and 51st Street a wailing woman sat on the curb and a policeman stood in the middle of the roadway surrounded by a crowd.

"There sure is something going on," my driver said.

And, indeed, there was, although one wouldn't have known it by the lack of turmoil in front of CBS. There were no more than the usual number of pedestrians going by and, showing my pass, I had no difficulty in gaining access to the seat of the hysteria which at that moment was sweeping most of the United States.

The broadcast had ended and the studio and corridors vibrated with chatter, as perturbed executives, attachés, officious page boys, and annoyed cops rushed about. I was informed that during the latter portion of the program the policemen, in response to the complaints, had marched into the glass-encased control room, and watched in disbelief as Orson and others of his Mercury troupe, in business and sports clothes, stood stoically before the microphones reading their scripts, ignorant of the havoc they were creating throughout the land.

When the executives and the law burst through the studio doors to confront him after the broadcast had come to its crashing finale, Welles was astounded to hear that listeners had taken his fantasy literally.

"How could they?" he said. "They were told several times it wasn't real."

"Have you any statement to make?" the newspapermen demanded.

"None whatsoever," he said, and ran with his cast from the studio down the corridor. The press followed, but before they could be intercepted, the Mercury troupe was downstairs and in the cabs that had been awaiting them. The reporters in other taxis pursued the fleeing performers, only to lose track of them in the maze of Times Square traffic. There, under the glow of sparkling lights, jittery thousands watched the *Times* electric sign for assurance that the "Martian invasion" had at last been repelled. The outwitted journalists then back-tracked to CBS, where a "network spokesman" solemnly promised that "such a thing will not happen again." At the *News* office the phones were still ringing, although the radio was making repeated announcements (until midnight) that Americans positively were in no peril from the spacemen.

So, on this Sunday evening of October 30, 1938, which was anything but "quiet," I not only had to do a complete rewrite of the column but also gave a hand in assembling items pouring in via telephones and teletypes. As these flooded the city and the telegraph desks, it became apparent that this was a startling story, with national and even international repercussions.

It had touched the movie theatre just around the corner, where scores had stampeded after a fear-crazed mother had pushed past the doorman to summon her husband and her child. "Get out! Get out!" she screamed. "The city's on fire! It had touched Harlem, where men and women had fallen to their knees in prayer . . . the Village, where crowds had converged on Washington Square . . . police stations throughout the city, besieged by frantic ones seeking refuge . . . upstate, Connecticut and, above all, New Jersey, where the "Martians" had landed. In that state's Trenton, Union City and other communities, thousands of fearful ones had taken to the streets and highways, and other foolhardy, curiosity-consumed hundreds in motor cars were still driving toward the spot where the "meteor" had crashed.

As the AP, UP, and the Chicago *Tribune* News Service wires in our office gave evidence, the panic's coils had also clutched most of the cities, towns, and hamlets from coast to coast and down south to the Mexican border. The people of the United States had succumbed to an unprecedented mass hysteria.

Immediately after the country had calmed its collective nerves, there were demands for government censorship of radio, but Washington wisely decided against such an un-American measure. After all, not only CBS but other networks had already decreed that thereafter no dramatic works should be broadcast which employed such realistic devices as news bulletins, flashes, or impersonations of public officials when these were of a kind to create uneasiness or panic.

It was said that this misstep would "ruin" Orson Welles; but instead, it won him a profitable national sponsor, and lifted him from a theatrical "wonder boy," admired only by a narrow circle, to the status of a national celebrity. Even today, despite his many other achievements, his name is synonymous to millions with the great "Martian invasion."

Political pundits, psychologists, psychiatrists, and other readers of the mass mind had a glorious time during the months that followed. The newspaper and the broadcasters of Hitler and Mussolini hailed the exhibition of hysteria as a sign of the decadence and cowardice of American democracy. Most of the native commentators attributed the incident to the climate of the times, which were truly hectic. The autumn of 1938 had witnessed one international crisis after another, and the world seemed to be on the verge of a mighty catastrophe.

"Is it surprising that this should have happened?" one analyst of public opinion asked. "Are not our imaginations so inflamed today that anything seems believable—no matter how fantastic?"

Those who gave serious thought to the episode also pointed out that broadcasting, improperly used by demagogues or dictators, could be one of the most dangerous weapons ever invented. And they called attention to the fact long recognized by the "trade": that a high percentage of those who tune in either do not listen attentively or do not hear accurately. Therefore, they said, major points must be repeated or emphasized several times. In other words, some of those obnoxious commercials which spell out each word and pound in their slogans are psychologically justified.

Three years after the Martians had made their foray against our planet, Pearl Harbor was bombed, but the excitement on that day did not approach the hysteria induced by Orson Wells. Observers explained that we had become so inured to tragedy it would be no longer possible to panic the American public. And, certainly, the stoical behavior of the British under the blitz gave them ground for such belief.

For a while, I agreed with them, but now I am not so sure. Just a few years ago, the Welles'-adaptation of *The War of the Worlds* was translated into Spanish and, with a few local touches added, broadcast over a Latin-American station. The reaction south of the border was even more violent than it had been in this country. The listeners not only gave way to hysteria, but, in an outburst of fury over having been "hoaxed," burned down the radio station and killed some of the actors!

And what of the United States? Suppose today we heard over the radio a bulletin that a troop of little men with death-ray guns had come forth from a flying saucer on some sandy waste in Arizona—just how calm would we be?

Who can give an accurate answer? Frankly, all I know is that back in 1938, Orson Welles and his "Men from Mars" ruined for one radio editor what might have been a quiet Sunday evening.

Questions

1. Orson Welles intended *The War of the Worlds* to:
   a. be a newsbroadcast
   b. a radio play
   c. promote his fame
   d. disturb the city's complacent activity

2. His play was received with _____.

3. The story is told by:
   a. Orson Welles
   b. reporter
   c. announcer of Broadcasting System
   d. CBS newsman

4. The reason listeners got upset was because they:
   a. made conclusions on only some of the information
   b. misinterpreted the words of Orson Welles and cast
   c. inferred facts from their own imagination
   d. none of the above

5. The radio program was about a:
   a. crashed meteor
   b. declaration of war
   c. martian invasion
   d. space fantasy

6. In response to the excitement of the radio broadcast:
   a. National Guard was called
   b. orders were issued to the army
   c. national emergency was proclaimed
   d. none of the above

7. According to the article the responses to the radio play were:
   a. numerous phone calls to the president
   b. panic-stricken crowds

    c. evacuation from the city

    d. none of the above.

8. The incident was:

    a. soon forgotten

    b. had international repercussions

    c. became a study for sociologists and psychologists

    d. b and c

9. This radio broadcast made Orson Welles:

    a. a national celebrity

    b. a laughingstock amongst producers

    c. a figure of scorn

    d. an outcast from radio productions

10. The lesson best learned from this incident is to listen
_____ and _____.

Answers

1.	b	6.	d
2.	hysteria	7.	b
3.	b	8.	d
4.	a	9.	a
5.	c	10.	attentively, and accurately

How did you do? How does your speed and comprehension, while using the Wiggle, compare to your reading while using the Z? Be sure that you have entered your words-per-minute rate and comprehension on your record sheet.

Practice the Wiggle again by reading for three more minutes in your novel. Record your words-per-minute rate and comprehension. Is there a difference this time? Did your rate go up? With practice and as you feel more comfortable each time that you use a new pacing pattern, your reading speed will have a tendency to go up. As you come to each new pacing pattern, practice it at least twice before moving on to the next pacing pattern.

Curve

When you feel comfortable with the Wiggle, practice the *Curve* shown in Fig. 3-2. The Curve is similar to the

Basic Z, but instead of the pacing finger moving directly along the lines of print in rather straight, rigid movements, the Curve is a relaxed, more flowing motion which rounds off the ends of the lines.

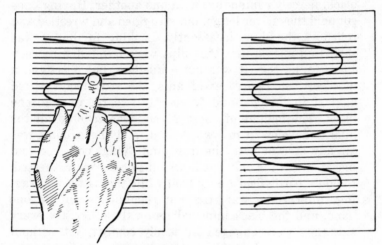

Fig. 3-2. Curve technique.

Remember, the eyes are not following the path of the curve, which is often cutting down into other lines, but are *reading along the lines of print*. Often, the movement of the Curve pattern is a couple of lines below where the eyes are reading but that movement is still visible and enables the eyes to keep moving, avoid regressions and unnecessarily long fixations. One more point to remember as you practice this new movement: relax. Only if you are relaxed as you read will you be able to get a true feeling about the effectiveness of each motion. Always enter your speed and comprehension for these readings on your record sheet.

After reading the next reading selection included here, practice the Curve while using your novel, or any other reading material. Practice the Curve until you feel comfortable using it. Practice this pacing movement in a five-minute drill. Calculate your words-per-minute rate and estimate your comprehension on your record sheet.

The Battle of the Ants*
by Henry David Thoreau

One day when I went out to my wood-pile, or rather my pile of stumps, I observed two large ants, the one red, the other much larger, nearly half an inch long, and black, fiercely contending with one another. Having once got hold they never let go, but struggled and wrestled and rolled on the chips incessantly. Looking farther, I was surprised to find that the chips were covered with such combatants, that it was not a *duellum*, but a *bellum*, a war between two races of ants, the red always pitted against the blacks, and frequently two red ones to one black. The legions of these Myrmidons covered all the hills and vales in my wood-yard, and the ground was already strewn with the dead and dying, both red and black. It was the only battle which I have ever witnessed, the only battle-field I ever trod while the battle was raging; internecine war; the red republicans on the one hand, and the black imperialists on the other. On every side they were engaged in deadly combat, yet without any noise that I could hear, and human soldiers never fought so resolutely. I watched a couple that were fast locked in each other's embraces, in a little sunny valley amid the chips, now at noonday prepared to fight till the sun went down, or life went out. The smaller red champion had fastened himself like a vice to his adversary's front, and through all the tumblings on that field never for an instant ceased to gnaw at one of his feelers near the root, having already caused the other to go by the board; while the stronger black one dashed him from side to side, and, as I saw on looking nearer, had already divested him of several of his members. They fought with more pertinacity than bulldogs. Neither manifested the least disposition to retreat. It was evident that their battle-cry was "Conquer or die." In the meanwhile there came along a single red ant on the hillside of this valley, evidently full of excitement, who either had despatched his foe, or

---

*From "Brute Neighbors," Chapter XII of *Walden.*

had not yet taken part in the battle; probably the latter, for he had lost none of his limbs; whose mother had charged him to return with his shield or upon it. Or perchance he was some Achilles, who had nourished his wrath apart, and had now come to avenge or rescue his Patroclus. He saw this unequal combat from afar—for the blacks were nearly twice the size of the red—he drew near with rapid pace till he stood on his guard within half an inch of the combatants; then, watching his opportunity, he sprang upon the black warrior, and commenced his operations near the root of his right fore leg, leaving the foe to select among his own members; and so there were three united for life, as if a new kind of attraction had been invented which put all other locks and cements to shame. I should not have wondered by this time to find that they had their respective musical bands stationed on some eminent chip, and playing their national airs the while, to excite the slow and cheer the dying combatants. I was myself excited somewhat even as if they had been men. The more you think of it, the less the difference. And certainly there is not the fight recorded in Concord history, at least, if in the history of America, that will bear a moment's comparison with this, whether for the numbers engaged in it, or for the patriotism and heroism displayed. For numbers and for carnage it was an Austerlitz or Dresden. Concord Fight! Two killed on the patriots' side, and Luther Blanchard wounded! Why here every ant was a Buttrick—"Fire! for God's sake fire!"—and thousands shared the fate of Davis and Hosmer. There was not one hireling there. I have no doubt that it was a principle they fought for, as much as our ancestors, and not to avoid a three-penny tax on their tea; and the results of this battle will be as important and memorable to those whom it concerns as those of the battle of Bunker Hill, at least.

I took up the chip on which the three I have particularly described were struggling, carried into my house, and placed it under a tumbler on my window-sill, in order to see the issue. Holding a microscope to the first-mentioned red ant, I saw that, though he was assiduously gnawing at the near fore leg of his enemy, having severed his remaining feeler, his own breast was all torn away, exposing what vitals he had there to the jaws of the black warrior, whose breastplate was apparently too thick for him to pierce; and the dark carbuncles of the sufferer's eyes shone with ferocity such as war only could excite. They struggled half an hour longer under the tumbler, and when I looked again the black soldier had severed the heads of his foes from their bodies, and the still living heads were hanging on either side of him like ghastly trophies at his saddle-bow, still apparently as firmly fastened as ever, and he was endeavoring with feeble struggles, being without feelers, and with only the remnant of a leg, and I know not how many other wounds, to divest himself of them; which at length, after half an hour more, he accomplished. I raised the glass, and he went off over the window-sill in that crippled state. Whether he finally survived that combat, and spent the remainder of his days in some Hôtel des Invalides, I do not know; but I thought that his industry would not be worth much thereafter. I never learned which party was victorious, nor the cause of the war, but I felt for the rest of that day as if I had my feelings excited and harrowed by witnessing the struggle, the ferocity and carnage, of a human battle before my door.

Kirby and Spence tell us that the battles of ants have long been celebrated and the date of them recorded, though they say that Huber is the only modern author who appears to have witnessed them. "Aeneas Sylvius," say they, "after giving a very circumstantial account of one contested with great obstinacy by a great and small species on the trunk of a pear tree," adds that " 'this action was fought in the pontificate of Eugenius the Fourth, in the presence of Nicholas Pistoriensis, an eminent lawyer, who related the whole history of the battle with the greatest fidelity.' A similar engagement between great and small ants is recorded by Olaus Magnus, in which the small ones, being victorious, are said to have buried the bodies of their own soldiers, but left those of their giant enemies a prey to the birds. This event happened previous to the expulsion of the tyrant Christiern the Second from Sweden." The battle which I witnessed took place in the Presidency of Polk, five years before the passage of Webster's Fugitive-Slave Bill.

Questions

1. The battle observed by the author took place in his:

    a. window sill
    b. garden
    c. wood pile
    d cupboard

2. The battle was:

    a. a duel between two ants
    b. a battle among like ants
    c. a war between two races of ants
    d. none of the above

3. The author likens the two factions to:

    a. whigs and tories
    b. republicans and democrats
    c. doves and hawks
    d. republicans and imperialists

4. Their battlecry appeared to be:

    a. Conquer or die!
    b. A fight to the finish!
    c. May the best ant win!
    c. none of the above

5. He likens the newcomer to:

    a. Achilles
    b. Patroclus
    c. Davis
    d. Hosmer

6. The newcomer:

    a. circled until he got into a good battle position
    b. joined the battle in process between a red ant and a black ant
    c. stayed on the edges of the battlefield where it was safe
    d. killed more of the enemy than any other ant

7. The author compares the numbers, patriotism and heroism to that shown at:

    a. Valley Forge
    b. Concord
    c. Bunker Hill
    d. Gettysburg

8. The battle recounted took place:

    a. at the time of the Emancipation Proclamation
    b. during the Presidency of Polk
    c. five years after the Fugitive-Slave Bill
    d. at the time of the expulsion of Christiern the Second from Sweden

9. The author examined the battling ants:

    a. by placing them on a mirror
    b. with a magnifying glass
    c. through a small telescope
    d. through a microscope

10. The only modern author to witness a battle of ants is said to be:

    a. Kirby
    b. Spence
    c. Huber
    d. Pistoriensis

Answers

1. c	5. a	9. d
2. c	6. b	10. c
3. d	7. b	
4. a	8. b	

Loop

Another pacing movement is the *Loop,* which will rapidly increase your speed. First look at the illustration of the loop in Fig. 3-3 and then read the description of its application.

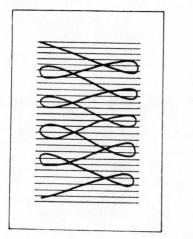 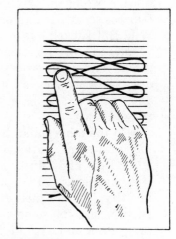

Fig. 3-3. Loop technique.

As with the Z and Curve this movement is done with the index finger and is a relaxed gliding of the finger across the line and then, instead of curving down at the end of the line, looping up and back to the beginning of the second line where a second upward loop is made to reverse direction and start reading across the next line. CAUTION: the loops at the beginning and ending of each line should be very small. In fact, for those who prefer the loop, there is a tendency to develop something of a swinging, back-and-forth effect in pacing. Before you try this on your reading selection you may want to trace over the Loop pattern several times on the illustration.

Be certain that you have recorded your reading score from the last reading selection. Then practice the Loop pacing movement in the following reading selection. After completing this, practice in your novel for several minutes.

Steer Clear of the Grizzly*
by Jack Denton Scott

There is stark evidence that our grizzly bear, once branded with the name *Ursus horribilis* (horrible bear), endeavored to live up to it: It sent Meriwether Lewis (intrepid partner in that famed Lewis and Clark Expedition) howling in terror into the Missouri River, chased fearless scout Kit Carson up a tree, and put ace gunman Wild Bill Hickok out of action for nearly a year.

Even before its scientific name was dry on paper, the grizzly had been recorded crushing a buffalo's head with one blow, carrying off an 800-pound elk without effort, and easily dragging a 1,300-pound moose a mile over rough country.

On the other hand, three grizzlies I saw not long ago in Yellowstone National Park after much patient work with legs and binoculars, could have been renamed Brownie Scouts. Like all grizzlies, they were easy to identify. Though their fur varied from cocoa, reddish to rusty-black (in some areas they are straw-yellow, or gray, even an off-white in the Far North) they had the distinctive humped shoulders, the mane, dish face, long, and slightly upturned snout. Even from a distance the huge, muscled bodies promised immense strength. But they were shy as mountain sheep. They reconnoitered carefully from a distance, retreated when I advanced, and generally gave an overall impression of, if not outright timidity, at least an over-developed sense of caution.

With good reason: Those bears I saw are among less than 1,000 of their mighty race (exclusive of Alaska) left in the United States. Former president Theodore Roosevelt succinctly summed up the reason for both the grizzly bear's caution and its sadly decreased numbers.

He called it King of Game Beasts, the mighty lord of the wilderness, adding, "He has been hunted for sport,

---

*Jack Denton Scott, "Steer Clear of the Grizzly," *National Wildlife Magazine*, June/July 1971, vol. 9, pp. 13-15. Copyright 1971 by the National Wildlife Federation.

and hunted for his pelt, and hunted for the bounty, and hunted as a dangerous animal to livestock, until save in the wildest districts, he has learned to be more wary than a deer, and to avoid man's presence almost as carefully as the most timid game."

When white men first arrived in North America, the grizzly didn't have too much trouble avoiding their presence. It is believed the grizzlies have been here for one million years and that there were well over 100,000 of them ranging from the great western plains to the Pacific, from Canada to Mexico, during the early settlement of the country. Adaptable, the grizzly took grassland, swamps, deserts, mountains, forests in its stride. With such vast range, the bear could avoid most men, especially the newcomers. Indians had an inbred respect for the grizzly, and whenever possible, left it strictly alone.

They knew its merits included not only great strength, but keen senses of scenting and hearing (eyesight is poor), a high intelligence, the ability to run almost as fast as deer over rough country (bears have been clocked making 30 miles per hour in bursts of speed); the grizzly could swim nearly as well as a beaver, and its six-inch claws (five on each foot) were hard and sharp as French boning knives, and could partially skin a man with one swipe. When surprised by bands of hunting Indians it has been recorded that it took six braves to down a grizzly, and that Sioux would give up wives before they would their grizzly teeth-and-claw necklaces. So the bear had quite a reputation when the pioneers arrived and pushed west in a locust spread.

The grizzly was almost a match for them. Like range, food was not at first a problem, though through disrupted ecology, it became one. Classified as carnivorous, the bear eats less flesh than a wolf or a fox. It gives a new dimension to the word omnivorous, not only feasting on anything from a mouse to a moose, but nearly anything in between as an appetizer, ranging the appetite alphabet from ant to zooplankton—tiny aquatic animal life that the bears scoop off water surfaces. In the spring they feed on new grass, chopping contentedly as cattle; they have been observed sitting like men stripping wild berry bushes, and they will dig a hole larger than themselves to pounce on a vole or a mole, then sit like club gentlemen, daintily picking their teeth with a front claw. Those claws also make grizzlies skilled fishermen. They use them almost like hands to flip salmon out of streams.

Civilization defeated grizzly. What defeated the grizzly was hungry civilization, eating voraciously at the wilderness. The fiercest of the grizzlies was the great plains species for it did not have the retreats of the mountain or forest bears, and when it was surprised, wounded, or cornered, it came out fighting. It gave all species of grizzlies a bad name. It did pretty well too, until the advent of the Sharps rifle in the 1850s. This not only finished wiping out the buffalo (on which the plains grizzly sometimes fed) but it weighed the battle in the favor of man, the big bear's only real rival. Disease didn't seem to touch the grizzly, and other than sometimes having decayed teeth, its only weakness was the porcupine. The bear loves their flesh and in its desire for it sometimes neglects to flip the animals over on their backs to avoid the quills and gets a mouthful that fester and infect and cause the bear to die of starvation.

But cattle really sealed the grizzly's doom. They replaced buffalo on the plains, and the bears often took them. They were easy to kill, tasted about the same as buffalo and roamed the same unfenced areas. This put a price on the grizzly's head. One, Old Mose, ranchers claimed had killed five men and over 500 cattle, had a $1,000 price tag, and cleverly eluded pursuers for quite a while, using its grizzly talents of backtracking and lying submerged in water. That prize bounty on him was finally paid, but the going price for a grizzly scalp was $10. Bounties were greedily collected: often hunters collected as many as 100 scalps per man. Five trappers returned from a year in Oregon with 700 grizzly scalps and pelts.

Female grizzlies mate at three years, and breed every two years, usually producing no more than two cubs, thus their population has never been large. Courtship is from June to August, with the bears sometimes tenderly embracing, sitting like teenage lovers hugging. But sometimes it get rough and males will fight over a mate. The female has been known to rush in, whip them both, then make its own choice.

Dens are dug or found on high ground where they will be dry, bedded with leaves and grass, and the bears retire for the winter, separately. They hole up in late fall and emerge in early spring, depending upon locale. After emerging from their winter dens, grizzlies have been observed limbering up by jogging in place like a man. Their denning up is not true hibernation: there is little change in body temperature, or in the tempo of breathing or pulse. Often during mild winters bears have been seen out of their dens. The twin cubs are usually whelped in the den in February after 226 days. They are born blind, almost hairless, toothless, eight inches long, weighing about 24 ounces, looking like kittens.

Cubs mature at eight. The cubs venture from the den at two months, in April or May. In another three months they are helping with the groceries, but even then they nurse right through the summer. They are tutored from the moment they leave the den, their mother a stern teacher, slapping or pushing her cubs to emphasize lessons. One observer saw a female slap a cub and send it spinning four feet from a rattlesnake. The young stay with mother for two years, leaving her in September. They mature at eight; it is not unusual for a grizzly to live for 30 years.

Grizzlies (other than the two-year family grouping) are solitary, live-and-let-live creatures who guard their own food range of nine square miles, but rarely are spoiling for a fight. If startled, wounded or come upon suddenly, they will kill humans. Several horrible incidents in recent years point up the need for extreme caution while camping or hiking in grizzly country.

Most naturalists with whom I have talked do not believe the grizzly deserves the bad reputation it has acquired. Among them is Sally Carrighar who ably states the bear's case in *Wild Heritage.*

She and other experts believe that as a species the grizzlies have been hunted so much that to them the smell of man and his gun is that of a predator out to kill. Joseph Dixon, naturalist of the National Park Service, claims that most wild animals know the odor of guns and ammunition. They are aware that guns are used for killing, and when they scent them their protective fighting instincts are aroused.

This could be the reason for one of the most bizarre grizzly attacks ever recorded. Jack O'Connor (in *The Art of Hunting Big Game*) tells of what happened to his friend, Field Johnson, a Yukon Indian guide, in the spring of 1950. He was hunting for moose with an old .30-.30 carbine, walking in the bush, when he was struck from behind with such a tremendous blow that his rifle went flying, and he somersaulted, head over heels.

Groggy, he soon realized that a grizzly was mauling him. He played dead, hoping the bear would give up and go away. Finally the grizzly did. But first it dug a hole and buried Johnson. Bleeding, in pain; Johnson lay there listening to the bear sniffing and moving around. He believed that it stayed there for an hour, then not hearing the bear, he dug himself out of the dirt and brush.

As he staggered to his feet, the grizzly rushed out of the brush where it had been hiding and cuffed Johnson to the ground again, biting and dragging him a half-mile. Conscious only part of the time, Johnson felt himself being buried again. This time in a deeper hole. Many hours later, in great pain, Johnson regained consciousness, got out of his second grave and somehow made it to the Alaskan Highway and into Whitehorse. He survived, but later went insane.

Burying their prey or enemies seems to be the custom of grizzlies and their close relatives the brown bears. Ben

Berg, a friend with whom I had shared adventures in Spitzbergen, Norway, not long ago, was photographing salmon jumping in the Brooks River, near King Salmon in Alaska. Ben was putting the action of two fishermen and the leaping salmon on 16-mm color film when a bear came and joined the fun. The 500-pound animal caught and calmly ate its fill of salmon, napped on the bank of the river for awhile, then awoke and sat in the river watching the fishermen whip their flyrods.

Camera still in action, Ben and his companion were startled and frightened to see a bear about twice the size of the peaceful spectator suddenly come down a steep slope, stand up behind the smaller bear, then attack. One hundred yards away, Ben stayed with his camera, recording the large bear literally tearing the other to pieces, disemboweling, then drowning him. Finally, the big bear dragged the other out of the river, up a 25-foot embankment and buried him.

Were Ben Berg's bears grizzlies? This leads to heated discussion. There is no question but that the grizzly is a distinct species, albeit a complicated one: Respected naturalist Victor H. Cahalane (who wrote the animal bible, *Mammals of North America*), formerly chief biologist of our national parks, states flatly, "the grizzly bear is the largest carnivore on earth. Its family includes the big brown, giant Alaska (Kodiak) and the off-white barren ground bears." Cahalane's size yardstick: grizzly length can run from five to nine feet, from 300 to well over 1,000 pounds.

Some naturalists believe Alaskan brown bears are a separate species (one weighed 1,656 pounds), not grizzlies. I shall not intrude opinion except to further cite Mr. Calahane.

He claims that grizzlies often differ in appearance, even to shape of skull and teeth, and that these disparate bears may have the same range and even mate with one another. Cahalane has also discovered that bears with the same coat, head, claws and identity, can be found 1,000 miles from their normal range.

"One scientist," Cahalane says, "has described no less than 84 species and subspecies of grizzlies and big brown bears in North America, including five distinct species on one island only 100 miles long and 20 miles wide. Probably no other piece of research has brought dignified mammalogists nearer to name-calling and nose-punching than the question of correctly classifying grizzly bears."

Grizzlies vary in size. One fact is certain: grizzlies vary considerably in size, depending upon locale. The smallest, the Sonora, not much larger than the black bear, ranged in or near Mexico; the largest, called the Tejon or California, nearly the size of the "Alaskan Brown," had its home-ground in California, and the great plains. This one was also called the great plains and "silvertip" because of the grizzled appearance caused by white-tipped guard hairs. Both of these types are now extinct, as are 16 other geographic forms.

Right now, except for those in Yellowstone, Glacier and Teton national parks, there are few grizzlies left in the United States. At the north entrance of Yellowstone in Montana, grizzly bears are sighted every year. In fact, there is a hunting season on them. It is claimed that there are also grizzlies in Washington, Wyoming, the San Juan mountains of Colorado, and the Marshall Wilderness in Montana. But none have been sighted in these areas in some time. It is estimated (and disputed by many experts as an over-optimistic figure which lumps together all species of brown bears) that there may be as many as 10,000 in Alaska, and the big brown bears are still doing quite well in British Columbia, Yukon, and the Northwest Territories.

A bronze statue has been erected to what many natural scientists call our greatest bear near the Natural History Museum in Denver, Colorado. Called "The Grizzly's Last Stand," a female stands guarding twin cubs, an inscription in stone beneath it:

When the Grizzly is gone we shall have lost the most sublime specimen of wildlife that exalts the western wilderness.

An epitaph?

Questions

1. Among the three historic figures mentioned as having encountered a grizzly was:

   a. Kit Carson
   b. Buffalo Bill
   c. Davy Crockett
   d. William Clark

2. The grizzly's fur may be:

   a. rusty black
   b. straw yellow
   c. gray
   d. all of the above

3. There are less than _____ of these bears left in the Continental United States.

   a. 800
   b. 500
   c. 1,000
   d. 10,000

4. It is believed that grizzlies have been in North America for _____ years.

5. The grizzly's merits do *not* include:

   a. great strength
   b. high intelligence
   c. keen eyesight
   d. great speed

6. The grizzly can best be described as:

   a. carnivorous
   b. omnivorous
   c. insectivorous
   d. herbivorous

7. Female grizzlies mate at:

   a. two years
   b. three years
   c. eight years
   d. ten years

8. A custom of grizzlies seems to be:

   a. burying their enemies
   b. drowning their enemies and prey
   c. skinning their prey
   d. eating their enemies

9. One scientist has described _____ species and subspecies of grizzlies and big brown bears in North America.

   a. 20
   b. 30
   c. 84
   d. 100

10. Most of the remaining grizzlies in the United States can be found in:

   a. Yellowstone, Glacier, and Teton National Parks
   b. Washington and Wyoming
   c. San Juan Mountains
   d. Marshall Wilderness

Answers

1. a	5. c	9. c
2. d	6. b	10. a
3. c	7. b	
4. d	8. a	

The Loop has become a favorite pacing motion because it is relaxing and still allows for a high speed in reading. Check to see how rapidly you can read using the Loop in a five-minute drill in your novel. Record your score and comprehension and compare it with your other reading rates. By the way, don't be discouraged if your progress chart seems to be fluctuating—that's normal. Depending on things like the interest, familiarity, and degree of fatigue, your score will go up and down. It is important to watch the *trend* of your scores. That should be going up. Begin reading.

Arrow

After you have recorded your score for the Loop, try the *Arrow* pacing motion as shown below in Fig. 3-4.

In moving the finger straight down the page your eyes are still reading across the line, but are being pulled from

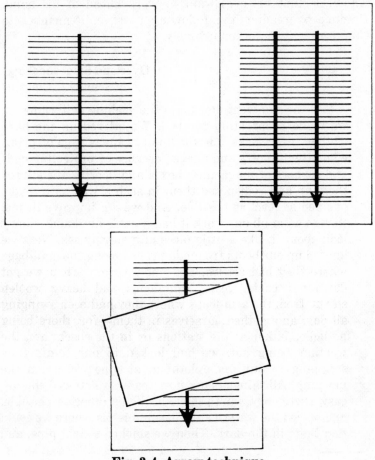

Fig. 3-4. Arrow technique.

line to line at a steady pace. The Arrow can be practiced
with one or two fingers, down the center or margins of the
page. Or, instead of your fingers, you can use a card, ruler,
or straight edge. If you use a card, try slanting the left
corner of the card at an angle that exposes the beginning
of each new line. As you pull the card down, the tilted card
acts as a very effective pacer, in effect pulling your eyes
across the line as well as down the page. This pacing movement is for the individual who feels uncomfortable with a
lot of movement on the page as he reads, or for the person
who feels that his eyes want to work ahead of his hand.
Practice by reading the following passage. Remember to
time yourself. Begin immediately.

Overland Stagecoaching*
by Samuel L. Clemens

As the sun went down and the evening chill came on,
we made preparation for bed. We stirred up the hard
leather letter-sacks, and the knotty canvas bags of printed matter (knotty and uneven because of projecting ends
and corners of magazines, boxes and books). We stirred
them up and redisposed them in such a way as to make
our bed as level as possible. And we *did* improve it, too,
though after all our work it had an upheaved and billowy
look about it, like a little piece of a stormy sea. Next we
hunted up our boots from odd nooks among the mail-bags
where they had settled, and put them on. Then we got
down our coats, vests, pantaloons and heavy woolen
shirts, from the arm-loops where they had been swinging
all day, and clothed ourselves in them—for, there being
no ladies either at the stations or in the coach, and the
weather being hot, we had looked to our comfort by
stripping to our underclothing, at nine o'clock in the
morning. All things being now ready, we stowed the uneasy Dictionary where it would lie as quiet as possible,
and placed the water-canteens and pistols where we could
find them in the dark. Then we smoked a final pipe, and

*From Chap. VI of *Roughing It.*

swapped a final yarn; after which, we put the pipes, tobacco and bag of coin in snug holes and caves among the mail-bags, and then fastened down the coach curtains all around, and made the place as "dark as the inside of a cow," as the conductor phrased it in his picturesque way. It was certainly as dark as any place could be— nothing was even dimly visible in it. And finally, we rolled ourselves up like silk-worms, each person in his own blanket, and sank peacefully to sleep.

Whenever the stage stopped to change horses, we would wake up and try to recollect where we were—and succeed—and in a minute or two the stage would be off again, and we likewise. We began to get into country, now, threaded here and there with little streams. These had high, steep banks on each side, and every time we flew down one bank and scrambled up the other, our party inside got mixed somewhat. First we would all be down in a pile at the forward end of the stage, nearly in a sitting posture, and in a second we would shoot to the other end, and stand on our heads. And we would sprawl and kick, too, and ward off ends and corners of mail-bags that came lumbering over us and about us; and as the dust rose from the tumult, we would all sneeze in chorus, and the majority of us would grumble, and probably say some hasty thing, like: "Take your elbow out of my ribs! Can't you quit crowding?"

Every time we avalanched from one end of the stage to the other, the Unabridged Dictionary would come too; and every time it came it damaged somebody. One trip it "barked" the Secretary's elbow; the next trip it hurt me in the stomach, and the third it tilted Bemis's nose up till he could look down his nostrils—he said. The pistols and coin soon settled to the bottom, but the pipes, pipe-stems, tobacco and canteens clattered and floundered after the Dictionary every time it made an assault on us, and aided and abetted the book by spilling tobacco in our eyes, and water down our backs.

Still, all things considered, it was a very comfortable night. It wore gradually away, and when at last a cold gray light was visible through the puckers and chinks in the curtains, we yawned and stretched with satisfaction, shed our cocoons, and felt that we had slept as much as was necessary. By and by, as the sun rose up and warmed the world, we pulled off our clothes and got ready for breakfast. We were just pleasantly in time, for five minutes afterward the driver sent the weird music of his bugle winding over the grassy solitudes, and presently we detected a low hut or two in the distance. Then the rattling of the coach, the clatter of our six horses' hoofs, and the driver's crisp commands, awoke to a louder and stronger emphasis, and we went sweeping down on the station at our smartest speed. It was fascinating—that old overland stagecoaching.

We jumped out in undress uniform. The driver tossed his gathered reins out on the ground, gaped and stretched complacently, drew off his heavy buckskin gloves with great deliberation and insufferable dignity—taking not the slightest notice of a dozen solicitious inquiries after his health, and humbly facetious and flattering accostings, and obsequious tenders of service, from five or six hairy and half-civilized station-keepers and hostlers who were nimbly unhitching our steeds and bringing the fresh team out of the stables—for in the eyes of the stage-driver of that day, station-keepers and hostlers were a sort of good enough low creatures, useful in their place, and helping to make up a world, but not the kind of beings which a person of distinction could afford to concern himself with; while, on the contrary, in the eyes of the station-keeper and the hostler, the stage-driver was a hero—a great and shining dignitary, the world's favorite son, the envy of the people, the observed of the nations. When they spoke to him they received his insolent silence meekly, and as being the natural and proper conduct of so great a man; when he opened his lips they all hung on his words with admiration (he never honored a particular individual with a remark, but addressed it with a broad generality to the horses, the stables, the surrounding country *and* the human underlings); when

he discharged a facetious insulting personality at a
hostler, that hostler was happy for the day; when he
uttered his one jest—old as the hills, coarse, profane,
witless, and inflicted on the same audience, in the same
language, every time his coach drove up there—the var-
lets roared, and slapped their thighs, and swore it was
the best thing they'd ever heard in all their lives. And how
they would fly around when he wanted a basin of water,
a gourd of the same, or a light for his pipe—but they
would instantly insult a passenger if he so far forgot
himself as to crave a favor at their hands. They could
do that sort of insolence as well as the driver they copied
it from—for, let it be borne in mind, the overland driver
had but little less contempt for his passengers than he
had for his hostlers.

The hostlers and station-keepers treated the really
powerful *conductor* of the coach merely with the best of
what was their idea of civility, but the *driver* was the only
being they bowed down to and worshipped. How ad-
miringly they would gaze up at him in his high seat as he
gloved himself with lingering deliberation, while some
happy hostler held the bunch of reins aloft, and waited
patiently for him to take it! And how they would bom-
bard him with glorifying ejaculations as he cracked his
long whip and went careening away.

The station buildings were long, low huts, made of
sun-dried mud-colored bricks, laid up without mortar
(*adobes*, the Spaniards called these bricks, and Americans shorten it to *'dobies*). The roofs, which had no slant
to them worth speaking of, were thatched and then sodded
or covered with a thick layer of earth, and from this
sprung a pretty rank growth of weeds and grass. It was
the first time we had ever seen a man's front yard on top
of his house. The buildings consisted of barns, stable-
room for twelve or fifteen horses, and a hut for an eating
room for passengers. This latter had bunks in it for the
station-keeper and a hostler or two. You could rest your
elbows on its eaves, and you had to bend in order to get
in at the door. In place of a window there was a square

hole about large enough for a man to crawl through, but this had no glass in it. There was no flooring, but the ground was packed hard. There was no stove, but the fireplace served all needful purposes. There were no shelves, no cupboards, no closets. In a corner stood an open sack of flour, and nestling against its base were a couple of black and venerable tin coffee-pots, a tin tea-pot, a little bag of salt, and a side of bacon.

By the door of the station-keeper's den, outside, was a tin wash-basin, on the ground. Near it was a pail of water and a piece of yellow bar soap, and from the eaves hung a hoary blue woolen shirt, significantly—but this latter was the station-keeper's private towel, and only two persons in all the party might venture to use it—the stage-driver and the conductor. The latter would not, from a sense of decency; the former would not because he did not choose to encourage the advances of a station-keeper. We had towels—in the valise; they might as well have been in Sodom and Gomorrah. We (and the conductor) used our handkerchiefs, and the driver his pantaloons and sleeves. By the door, inside, was fastened a small old-fashioned looking-glass frame, with two little fragments of the original mirror lodged down in one corner of it. This arrangement afforded a pleasant double-barreled portrait of you when you looked into it, with one half of your head set up a couple of inches above the other half. From the glass frame hung the half of a comb by a string—but if I had to describe that patriarch or die, I believe I would order some sample coffins. It had come down from Esau and Samson, and had been accumulating hair ever since—along with certain impurities. In one corner of the room stood three or four rifles and muskets, together with horns and pouches of ammunition. The station-men wore pantaloons of coarse, country-woven stuff, and into the seat and inside of the legs were sewed ample additions of buckskin, to do duty in place of leggings, when the man rode horseback—so the pants were half dull blue and half yellow, and unspeakably picturesque. The pants were stuffed into the tops of high boots, the heels whereof were armed with great Spanish spurs, whose little iron clogs and chains jingled with every step. The man wore a huge beard and mustachios, an old slouch hat, a blue woolen shirt, no suspenders, no vest, no coat—in a leather sheath in his belt, a great long "navy" revolver (slung on right side, hammer to the front), and projecting from his boot a horn-handled bowie-knife. The furniture of the hut was neither gorgeous nor much in the way. The rocking-chairs and sofas were not present and never had been, but they were represented by two three-legged stools, a pine-board bench four feet long, and two empty candle-boxes. The table was a greasy board on stilts, and the table-cloth and napkins had not come—and they were not looking for them, either. A battered tin platter, a knife and fork, and a tin pint cup, were at each man's place, and the driver had a queensware saucer that had seen better days. Of course this duke sat at the head of the table. There was one isolated piece of table furniture that bore about it a touching air of grandeur in misfortune. This was the caster. It was German silver, and crippled and rusty, but it was so preposterously out of place there it was suggestive of a tattered exiled king among barbarians, and the majesty of its native position compelled respect even in its degradation. There was only one cruet left, and that was a stopperless, fly-specked broken-necked thing, with two inches of vinegar in it, and a dozen preserved flies with their heels up and looking sorry they had invested there.

The station-keeper up-ended a disk of last week's bread, of the shape and size of an old-time cheese, and carved some slabs from it which were as good as Nicholson pavement, and tenderer.

He sliced off a piece of bacon for each man, but only the experienced old hands made out to eat it, for it was condemned army bacon which the United States would not feed to its soldiers in the forts, and the stage company had bought it cheap for the sustenance of their passengers and employes. We may have found this condemned army bacon further out on the plains than the section I am locating it in, but we *found* it—there is no gainsaying that.

Then he poured for us a beverage which he called *"Slumgullion,"* and it is hard to think he was not inspired when he named it. It really pretended to be tea, but there was too much dish-rag, and sand, and old bacon-rind in it to deceive the intelligent traveler. He had no sugar and no milk—not even a spoon to stir the ingredients with.

We could not eat the bread or the meat, nor drink the "slumgullion." And when I looked at that melancholy vinegar cruet, I thought of the anecdote (a very, very old one, even at that day) of the traveler who sat down to a table which had nothing on it but a mackerel and a pot of mustard. He asked the landlord if this was all. The landlord said:

"All! Why, thunder and lightning, I should think there was mackerel enough there for six."

"But I don't like mackerel."

"Oh—then help yourself to the mustard."

In other days I had considered it a good, a very good, anecdote, but there was a dismal plausibility about it, here, that took all the humor out of it.

Our breakfast was before us, but our teeth were idle.

I tasted and smelt, and said I would take coffee, I believed. The station-boss stopped dead still, and glared at me speechless. At last, when he came to, he turned away and said, as one who communes with himself upon a matter too vast to grasp:

"Coffee! Well, if that don't go clean ahead of me, I'm d——d!"

We could not eat, and there was no conversation among the hostlers and herdsmen—we all sat at the same board. At least there was no conversation further than a single hurried request, now and then, from one employe to another. It was always in the same form, and always gruffly friendly. Its western freshness and novelty startled me, at first, and interested me, but it presently grew monotonous, and lost its charm. It was:

"Pass the bread, you son of a skunk!" No, I forget—skunk was not the word; it seems to me it was still stronger than that; I knew it was, in fact, but it is gone from my memory, apparently. However, it is no matter—probably it was too strong for print, anyway. It is the landmark in my memory which tells me where I first encountered the vigorous new vernacular of the occidental plains.

We gave up the breakfast, and paid our dollar apiece and went back to our mail-bag bed in the coach, and found comfort in our pipes. Right here we suffered the first diminution of our princely state. We left our six fine horses and took six mules in their place. But they were wild Mexican fellows, and a man had to stand at the head of each of them and hold him fast while the driver gloved and got himself ready. And when at last he grasped the reins and gave the word, the men sprung suddenly away from the mules' heads and the coach shot from the station as if it had been issued from a cannon. How the frantic animals did scamper! It was a fierce and furious gallop —and the gait never altered for a moment till we reeled off ten or twelve miles and swept up to the next collection of little station-huts and stables.

So we flew along all day. At 2 p.m. the belt of timber that fringes the North Platte and marks its windings through the vast level floor of the Plains came in sight. At 4 p.m. we crossed a branch of the river, and at 5 p.m. we crossed the Platte itself, and landed at Fort Kearney, *fifty-six hours out from St. Joe*—three hundred miles!

Questions

1. The bed of letter-sacks and canvas bags is compared to:

    a. rocky ground
    b. a feather bed
    c. a stormy sea
    d. a grassy meadow

2. The travelers were dressed in _____ during the day.

   a. suits
   b. army uniforms
   c. blankets
   d. their underwear

3. Clemens compared the travelers rolled in blankets to:

   a. silk worms
   b. bugs in rugs
   c. caterpillars in cocoons

4. The stagecoach was traveling through country threaded with:

   a. foothills
   b. streams
   c. mountains
   d. rivers

5. The object which did the most personal harm to the pasengers was:

   a. a canteen
   b. the mail bags
   c. the dictionary
   d. none of these

6. The hero of the station keeper and hostlers was:

   a. the conductor
   b. the stage driver
   c. the guard
   d. the pasengers

7. The station buildings were:

   a. log cabins
   b. sod dugouts
   c. adobes
   d. thatch huts

8. The buildings consisted of:

   a. barns
   b. stable-room for horses
   c. an eating-room for passengers
   d. all of these

9. The piece of table furniture that seemed out of place was:

   a. a silver Lazy Susan
   b. a queensware saucer
   c. a cruet
   d. a fork

10. "Slumgullion" was a form of:

    a. coffee
    b. liquor
    c. tea
    d. none of the above

Answers

1.	c	6.	b
2.	d	7.	c
3.	a	8.	d
4.	b	9.	a
5.	c	10.	c

Four More
Advanced Pacing Techniques

In the following section you will review four more pacing movements. Don't go any further, however, until you have spent much time practicing the last four comfort patterns. As you practice each movement on your novel and any other practice reading, you may find a pacing motion especially suited to your needs.

The four new pacing movements are called *Crosshatch*, *Zig-Zag*, *Spiral*, and *Hop*.

Crosshatch

The *Crosshatch* movement is a little bit different in that it may be done with two fingers. Fig. 4-1A shows the general pattern. Fig. 4-1B shows how to run your index finger in a relaxed movement across the page. Fig. 4-1C shows the return sweep being made with the second finger.

This motion looks a lot more complicated than it really is. With a slight flicking of two fingers (one finger across, a second finger back) you will find a relaxing pacing motion that may be particularly helpful in increasing your reading efficiency. Remember, your eyes still read every word. It doesn't matter what pattern is used, it simply provides "pull" and rhythm for your eye movement.

After practicing the Crosshatch for a few minutes, or until you can pace fairly comfortably, read the next selection in this book. Afterward, read in your novel. Time

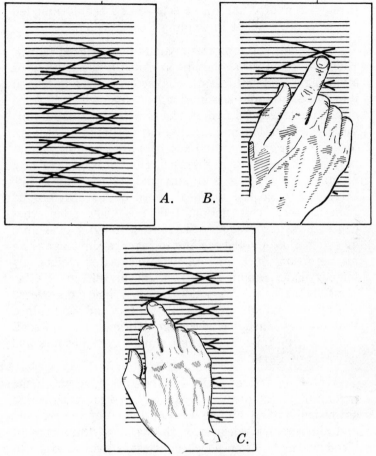

Fig. 4-1. Crosshatch movement.

yourself for five minutes. Enter your speed and comprehension on your record sheet.

Adventure of the German Student
by Washington Irving

On a stormy night, in the tempestuous times of the French revolution, a young German was returning to his lodgings, at a late hour, across the old part of Paris. The lightning gleamed, and the loud claps of thunder rattled through the lofty narrow streets—but I should first tell you something about this young German.

Gottfried Wolfgang was a young man of good family. He had studied for some time at Gottingen, but being of a visionary and enthusiastic character, he had wandered into those wild and speculative doctrines which have so often bewildered German students. His secluded life, his intense application, and the singular nature of his studies, had an effect on both mind and body. His health was impaired; his imagination diseased. He had been indulging in fanciful speculations on spiritual essences, until, like Swedenborg, he had an ideal world of his own around him. He took up a notion, I do not know from what cause, that there was an evil influence hanging over him; an evil genius or spirit seeking to ensnare him and ensure his perdition. Such an idea working on his melancholy temperament, produce the most gloomy effects. He became haggard and desponding. His friends discovered the mental malady preying upon him, and determined that the best cure was a change of scene; he was sent, therefore, to finish his studies amidst the splendors and gayeties of Paris.

Wolfgang arrived at Paris at the breaking out of the revolution. The popular delirium at first caught his enthusiastic mind, and he was captivated by the political and philosophical theories of the day: but the scenes of blood which followed shocked his sensitive nature, disgusted him with society and the world, and made him more than ever a recluse. He shut himself up in a solitary apartment in the *Pays Latin,* the quarter of students. There, in a gloomy street not far from the monastic walls of the Sorbonne, he pursued his favorite speculations. Sometimes he spent hours together in the great libraries of Paris, those catacombs of departed authors, rummaging among their hoards of dusty and obsolete works in quest of food for his unhealthy appetite. He was, in a manner, a literary ghoul, feeding in the charnel-house of decayed literature.

Wolfgang, though solitary and recluse, was of an ardent temperament, but for a time it operated merely upon his imagination. He was too shy and ignorant of the world to make any advances to the fair, but he was a passionate admirer of female beauty, and in his lonely chamber would often lose himself in reveries on forms and faces which he had seen, and his fancy would deck out images of loveliness far surpassing the reality.

While his mind was in this excited and sublimated state, a dream produced an extraordinary effect upon him. It was of a female face of transcendent beauty. So strong was the impression made, that he dreamt of it again and again. It haunted his thoughts by day, his slumbers by night; in fine, he became passionately enamoured of this shadow of a dream. This lasted so long that it became one of those fixed ideas which haunt the minds of melancholy men, and are at times mistaken for madness.

Such was Gottfried Wolfgang, and such his situation at the time I mentioned. He was returning home late one stormy night, through some of the old and gloomy streets of the *Marais*, the ancient part of Paris. The loud claps of thunder rattled among the high houses of the narrow streets. He came to the *Place de Grève*, the square where public executions are performed. The lightning quivered about the pinnacles of the ancient *Hôtel de Ville*, and shed flickering gleams over the open space in front. As Wolfgang was crossing the square, he shrank back with horror at finding himself close by the guillotine. It was the height of the reign of terror, when this dreadful instrument of death stood ever ready, and its scaffold was continually running with the blood of the virtuous and the brave. It had that very day been actively employed in the work of carnage, and there it stood in grim array, amidst a silent and sleeping city, waiting for fresh victims.

Wolfgang's heart sickened within him, and he was turning shuddering from the horrible engine, when he beheld a shadowy form, cowering as it were at the foot of the steps which led up to the scaffold. A succession of vivid flashes of lightning revealed it more distinctly. It was a female figure, dressed in black. She was seated on one of the lower steps of the scaffold, leaning forward, her face hid in her lap; and her long dishevelled tresses hanging to the ground, streaming with the rain which fell in torrents. Wolfgang paused. There was something awful in this solitary monument of woe. The female had the appearance of being above the common order. He knew the times to be full of vicissitude, and that many a fair head, which had once been pillowed on down, now wandered houseless. Perhaps this was some poor mourner whom the dreadful axe had rendered desolate, and who sat here heart-broken on the strand of existence, from which all that was dear to her had been launched into eternity.

He approached, and addressed her in the accents of sympathy. She raised her head and gazed wildly at him. What was his astonishment at beholding, by the bright glare of the lightning, the very face which had haunted him in his dreams. It was pale and disconsolate, but ravishingly beautiful.

Trembling, with violent and conflicting emotions, Wolfgang again accosted her. He spoke something of her being exposed at such an hour of the night, and to the fury of such a storm, and offered to conduct her to her friends. She pointed to the guillotine with a gesture of dreadful signification.

"I have no friend on earth!" said she.

"But you have a home," said Wolfgang.

"Yes—in the grave!"

The heart of the student melted at the words.

"If a stranger dare make an offer," said he, "without danger of being misunderstood, I would offer my humble dwelling as a shelter; myself as a devoted friend. I am friendless myself in Paris, and a stranger in the land; but if my life could be of service, it is at your disposal, and should be sacrificed before harm or indignity should come to you."

There was an honest earnestness in the young man's manner that had its effect. His foreign accent, too, was in his favor; it showed him not to be a hackneyed inhabitant of Paris. Indeed, there is an eloquence in true enthusiasm that is not to be doubted. The homeless stranger confided herself implicitly to the protection of the student.

He supported her faltering steps across the *Pont Neuf*, and by the place where the statue of Henry the Fourth had been overthrown by the populace. The storm had abated, and the thunder rumbled at a distance. All Paris was quiet; that great volcano of human passion slumbered for awhile, to gather fresh strength for the next day's eruption. The student conducted his charge through the ancient streets of the *Pays Latin*, and by the dusky walls of the Sorbonne, to the great dingy hotel which he inhabited. The old portress who admitted them stared with surprise at the unusual sight of the melancholy Wolfgang with a female companion.

On entering his apartment, the student, for the first time, blushed at the scantiness and indifference of his dwelling. He had but one chamber—an old-fashioned saloon—heavily carved, and fantastically furnished with the remains of former magnificence, for it was one of those hotels in the quarter of the Luxembourg palace, which had once belonged to nobility. It was lumbered with books and papers, and all the usual apparatus of a student, and his bed stood in a recess at one end.

When lights were brought, and Wolfgang had a better opportunity of contemplating the stranger, he was more than ever intoxicated by her beauty. Her face was pale, but of a dazzling fairness, set off by a profusion of raven hair that hung clustering about it. Her eyes were large and brilliant, with a singular expression approaching almost to wildness. As far as her black dress permitted her shape to be seen, it was of perfect symmetry. Her whole appearance was highly striking, though she was dressed in the simplest style. The only thing approaching to an ornament which she wore, was a broad black band round her neck, clasped by diamonds.

The perplexity now commenced with the student how to dispose of the helpless being thus thrown upon his protection. He thought of abandoning his chamber to her, and seeking shelter for himself elsewhere. Still he was so fascinated by her charms, there seemed to be such a spell upon his thoughts and senses, that he could not tear himself from her presence. Her manner, too, was singular and unaccountable. She spoke no more of the guillotine. Her grief had abated. The attentions of the student had first won her confidence, and then, apparently, her heart. She was evidently an enthusiast like himself, and enthusiasts soon understood each other.

In the infatuation of the moment, Wolfgang avowed his passion for her. He told her the story of his mysterious dream, and how she had possessed his heart before he had even seen her. She was strangely affected by his recital, and acknowledged to have an impulse towards him equally unaccountable. It was the time for wild theory and wild actions. Old prejudices and superstitions were done away; every thing was under the sway of the "Goddess of Reason." Among other rubbish of the old times, the forms and ceremonies of marriage began to be considered superfluous bonds for honorable minds. Social compacts were the vogue. Wolfgang was too much of a theorist not to be tainted by the liberal doctrines of the day.

"Why should we separate?" said he: "our hearts are united; in the eye of reason and honor we are as one. What need is there of sordid forms to bind high souls together?"

The stranger listened with emotion: she had evidently received illumination at the same school.

"You have no home nor family," continued he; "let me be every thing to you, or rather let us be every thing to one another. If form is necessary, form shall be observed—there is my hand. I pledge myself to you for ever."

"For ever?" said the stranger, solemnly.

"For ever!" repeated Wolfgang.

The stranger clasped the hand extended to her: "then I am yours," murmured she, and sank upon his bosom.

The next morning the student left his bride sleeping, and sallied forth at an early hour to seek more spacious apartments suitable to the change in his situation. When he returned, he found the stranger lying with her head hanging over the bed, and one arm thrown over it. He spoke to her, but received no reply. He advanced to awaken her from her uneasy posture. On taking her hand, it was cold—there was no pulsation—her face was pallid and ghastly.—In a word she was a corpse.

Horrified and frantic, he alarmed the house. A scene of confusion ensued. The police was summoned. As the officer of police entered the room, he started back on beholding the corpse.

"Good heaven!" cried he, "how did this woman come here?"

"Do you know anything about her?" said Wolfgang, eagerly.

"Do I?" exclaimed the officer: "she was guillotined yesterday."

He stepped forward; undid the black collar round the neck of the corpse, and the head rolled on the floor!

The student burst into a frenzy. "The fiend! the fiend has gained possession of me!" shrieked he: "I am lost for ever."

They tried to soothe him, but in vain. He was possessed with the frightful belief that an evil spirit had reanimated the dead body to ensnare him. He went distracted, and died in a mad-house.

Here the old gentleman with the haunted head finished his narrative.

"And is this really a fact?" said the inquisitive gentleman.

"A fact not to be doubted," replied the other. "I had it from the best authority. The student told it to me himself. I saw him in a mad-house in Paris."

Questions

1. The story takes place at the time of the:

   a. Revolutionary War
   b. World War I
   c. French Revolution
   d. French-Indian War

2. He came to what city to escape his melancholy?

   a. Paris
   b. Strasbourg
   c. Swedenborg
   d. Berlin

3. He believed his melancholic state was caused by:

   a. the oppression of the government
   b. the affluence of his parents
   c. his superior intelligence
   d. an evil spirit

4. The girl was visible:

   a. in the moonlight
   b. during the flashes of lightning
   c. because she held a candle
   d. in a lovely white dress

5. His reaction to her was:

   a. return her to her friends
   b. to get away from her as quickly as possible
   c. to take her to his apartment
   d. none of the above

6. Her appearance was:

   a. pale beauty, raven hair, large wild eyes
   b. closely cropped black hair and snapping black eyes
   c. fresh and young and innocent eyes
   d. dark and fearful

7. Her only adornment included:

   a. pearls
   b. gold

    c. rubies

    d. diamonds

8. Their passions were controlled by:

    a. The Goddess of Love

    b. The Goddess of Evil

    c. The Goddess of Reason

    d. The Goddess of Life

9. The happy couple was married:

    a. the night they met, by a Parish Priest

    b. two days later

    c. by pledging themselves to each other

    d. by a German theology student

10. Wolfgang's last days were spent:

    a. in a rest home for old gentlemen

    b. with a new bride

    c. at the home of his children

    d. in a mad-house

Answers

1. c	5. c	9. c
2. a	6. a	10. d
3. d	7. d	
4. b	8. c	

Zig-Zag

Do not let this next movement scare you if your comprehension is bad. This movement should not be used for your regular, normal reading because it is designed to cut down through lines, two at a time, and not to be used on line by line reading. There are occasions when you will want to read faster than line by line, but not quite at a skimming rate. Using the Zig-Zag pattern run your glance on an angle from the beginning of line one to the end of line two, to the beginning of line four, to the end of line six, and so on (Fig. 4-2). Doing this you will find that you will pick up large chunks of words and significant levels of comprehension. Later in the book this pacing pattern will be

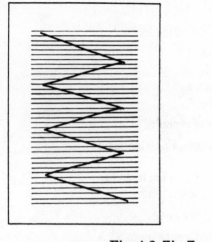 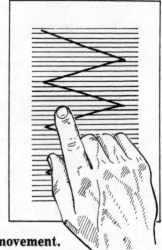

Fig. 4-2. Zig-Zag movement.

used in learning effective uses of skimming and scanning. For right now this pacing pattern is a good one to use if you are simply interested in getting a quick overview of some reading material.

Practice the Zig-Zag pacing movement for several minutes. Use this pattern while reading the next article. Then time yourself for five minutes as you use the Zig-Zag movement in your novel. How much do you remember of the contents reading in this manner?

The Young Deerslayer
by James Fenimore Cooper

It was an imposing scene into which Deerslayer now found himself advancing. All the older warriors were seated on the trunk of the fallen tree, waiting his approach with grave decorum. On the right stood the young men, armed, while the left was occupied by the women and children. In the center was an open space of considerable extent, always canopied by leaves, but from which the underbrush, dead wood, and other obstacles had been carefully removed. The more open area had probably been much used by former parties, for this was the place where the appearance of a sward was the most decided. The arches of the woods, even at high noon, cast their somber shadows on the spot, which the brilliant rays of the sun that struggled through the leaves contributed to mellow, and, if such an expression can be used, to illuminate. It was probably from a similar scene that the mind of man first got its idea of the effects of Gothic tracery and churchly hues; this temple of nature producing some such effect, so far as light and shadows were concerned, as the well-known offspring of human invention.

As was not unusual among the tribes and wandering bands of the aborigines, two chiefs shared, in nearly equal degrees, the principal and primitive authority that was wielded over these children of the forest. * * * One was a senior, well known for eloquence in debate, wisdom in council, and prudence in measures; while his great competitor, if not his rival, was a brave, distinguished in war, notorious for ferocity, and remarkable, in the way of intellect, for nothing but the cunning and expedients of the warpath. The first was Rivenoak, who has already been introduced to the reader, while the last was called le Panthère, in the language of the Canadas; or the Panther, to resort to the vernacular of the English colonies. The appellation of the fighting chief was supposed to indicate the qualities of the warrior, agreeably to a practice of the red-man's nomenclature; ferocity, cunning, and treachery being, perhaps, the distinctive features of his character. The title had been received from the French, and was prized so much the more from that circumstance, the Indian submitting profoundly to the greater intelligence of his pale-face allies in most things of this nature. How well the *sobriquet* was merited, will be seen in the sequel.

Rivenoak and the Panther sat side by side, awaiting the approach of their prisoner, as Deerslayer put his moccasined foot on the stand; nor did either move, or utter a syllable, until the young man had advanced into the center of the area, and proclaimed his presence with his voice. This was done firmly, though in the simple manner that marked the character of the individual.

"Here I am, Mingos," he said, in the dialect of the Delawares, a language that most present understood; "here I am, and there is the sun. One is not more true to the laws of natur', than the other has proved true to his word. I am your prisoner; do with me what you please. My business with man and 'arth is settled; nothing remains now but to meet the white man's God, accordin' to a white man's duties and gifts."

A murmur of approbation escaped even the women at this address, and, for an instant there was a strong and pretty general desire to adopt into the tribe one who owned so brave a spirit. Still there were dissenters from this wish, among the principal of whom might be classed the Panther, and his sister, le Sumach, so called from the number of her children, who was the widow of le Loup Cervier, now known to have fallen by the hand of the captive. Native ferocity held one in subjection, while the corroding passion of revenge prevented the other from admitting any gentler feeling at the moment. Not so with Rivenoak. This chief arose, stretched his arm before him in a gesture of courtesy, and paid his compliments with an ease and dignity that a prince might have envied. As, in that band, his wisdom and eloquence were confessedly without rivals, he knew that on himself would properly fall the duty of first replying to the speech of the pale-face.

"Pale-face, you are honest," said the Huron orator. "My people are happy in having captured a man, and not a skulking fox. We now know you; we shall treat you like a brave. If you have slain one of our warriors, and helped to kill others, you have a life of your own ready to give away in return. Some of my young men thought that the blood of a pale-face was too thin; that it would refuse to run under the Huron knife. You will show them it is not so; your heart is stout as well as your body. It is a pleasure to make such a prisoner; should my warriors say that the death of le Loup Cervier ought not to be forgotten, and that he cannot travel towards the land of spirits alone, that his enemy must be sent to overtake him, they will remember that he fell by the hand of a brave, and send you after him with such signs of our friendship as shall not make him ashamed to keep your company. I have spoken; you know what I have said."

"True enough, Mingo, all true as the gospel," returned the simple-minded hunter; "you *have* spoken, and I *do* know not only what you have *said*, but, what is still more important, what you *mean*. I dare to say your warrior the Lynx, was a stouthearted brave, and worthy of your fri'ndship and respect, but I do not feel unworthy to keep his company without any passport from your hands. Nevertheless, here I am, ready to receive judgment from your council, if, indeed, the matter was not determined among you afore I got back."

"My old men would not sit in council over a pale-face until they saw him among them," answered Rivenoak, looking around him a little ironically; "they said it would be like sitting in council over the winds; they go where they will, and come back as they see fit, and not otherwise. There was one voice that spoke in your favor, Deerslayer, but it was alone, like the song of the wren whose mate has been struck by the hawk."

"I thank that voice, whos'ever it may have been, Mingo, and will say it was a true voice as the rest were lying voices. A furlough is as binding on a pale-face, if he be honest, as it is on a red-skin; and was it not so, I would never bring disgrace on the Delawares, among whom I may be said to have received my edication. But words are useless and lead to braggin' feelin's; here I am; act your will on me."

Rivenoak made a sign of acquiescence, and then a short conference was privately held among the chiefs. As soon as the latter ended, three or four young men fell back from among the armed group, and disappeared. Then it was signified to the prisoner that he was at liberty to go at large on the point, until a council was held concerning his fate. * * *

In the meantime the business of the camp appeared to proceed in its regular train. The chiefs consulted apart, admitting no one but the Sumach to their councils; for she, the widow of the fallen warrior, had an exclusive right to be heard on such an occasion. The young men strolled about in indolent listlessness, awaiting the result with Indian patience, while the females prepared the feast that was to celebrate the termination of the affair, whether it proved fortunate, or otherwise, for our hero. No one betrayed feeling; and an indifferent observer, beyond the extreme watchfulness of the sentinels, would have detected no extraordinary movement or sensation to denote the real state of things. Two or three old women put their heads together, and, it appeared, un- favorably to the prospect of Deerslayer, by their scowling looks and angry gesture; but a group of Indian girls were evidently animated by a different impulse, as was appar- ent by stolen glances that expressed pity and regret. In this condition of the camp, an hour soon glided away.

Suspense is, perhaps, the feeling, of all others, that is most difficult to be supported. When Deerslayer landed, he fully, in the course of a few minutes, expected to undergo the tortures of an Indian revenge, and he was prepared to meet his fate manfully; but the delay proved far more trying than the nearer approach of suffering, and the intended victim began seriously to meditate some desperate effort at escape, as it might be from sheer anxiety to terminate the scene, when he was suddenly summoned to appear, once more, in front of his judges, who had already arranged the band in its former order, in readiness to receive him.

"Killer of the Deer," commenced Rivenoak, as soon as his captive stood before him, "my aged men have listened to wise words; they are ready to speak. You are a man whose fathers came from beyond the rising sun; we are children of the setting sun; we turn our faces towards the Great Sweet Lakes, when we look towards our villages. It may be a wise country and full of riches, towards the morning, but it is very pleasant towards the evening. We love most to look in that direction. When we gaze at the east, we feel afraid, canoe after canoe bringing more and more of your people in the track of the sun, as if their land was so full as to run over. The red-men are few already; they have need of help. One of our best lodges has lately been emptied by the death of its master; it will be a long time before his son can grow big enough to sit in his place. There is his widow; she will want venison to feed her and her children, for her sons are yet like the young of the robin before they quit the nest. By your hand has this great calamity befallen her. She has two duties; one to le Loup Cervier, and one to his children. Scalp for scalp, life for life, blood for blood, is one law; to feed her young, another. We know you, Killer of the Deer. You are honest; when you say a thing, it is so. You have but one tongue, and that is not forked, like a snake's. Your head is never hid in the grass; all can see it. What you say, that will you do. You are just. When you have done wrong, it is your wish to do right again, as soon as you can. Here is the Sumach; she is alone in her wigwam, with children crying around her for food; yonder is a rifle; it is loaded and ready to be fired. Take the gun; go forth and shoot a deer; bring the venison and lay it before the widow of le Loup Cervier; feed her children; call yourself her husband. After which, your heart will no longer be Delaware, but Huron; le Sumach's ears will not hear the cries of her children; my people will count the proper number of warriors."

"I feared this, Rivenoak," answered Deerslayer, when the other had ceased speaking; "yes, I did dread that it would come to this. Hows'ever, the truth is soon told, and that will put an end to all expectations on this head. Mingo, I'm white, and Christian-born; 'twould ill become me to take a wife, under red-skin forms, from among heathen. That which I wouldn't do in peaceable times, and under a bright sun, still less would I do behind clouds, in order to save my life. I may never marry; most likely Providence, in putting me up here in the woods, has intended I should live single, and without a lodge of my own; but should such a thing come to pass, none but a woman of my own color and gifts shall darken the door of my wigwam. As for feeding the young of your dead warrior, I would do that cheerfully, could it be done without discredit; but it cannot, seeing that I can never live in a Huron village. Your own young men must find the Sumach in venison, and the next time she marries, let her take a husband whose legs are not long enough to overrun territory that don't belong to him. We fou't a fair battle, and he fell; in this there is nothin' but what a brave expects, and should be ready to meet. As for getting a Mingo heart, as well might you expect to see grey hairs on a boy, or the blackberry growing on the pine. No, no, Huron; my gifts are white, so far as wives are consarned; it is Delaware in all things touchin' Indians."

These words were scarcely out of the mouth of Deerslayer, before a common murmur betrayed the dissatisfaction with which they had been heard. The aged women, in particular, were loud in their expressions of disgust; and the gentle Sumach herself, a woman quite old enough to be our hero's mother, was not the least pacific in her denunciations. But all the other manifestations of disappointment and discontent were thrown into the background by the fierce resentment of the Panther. This grim chief had thought it a degradation to permit his sister to become the wife of a pale-face of the Yengeese at all. * * * The animal from which he got his name does not glare on his intended prey with more frightful ferocity than his eyes gleamed on the captive; nor was his arm backward in seconding the fierce resentment that almost consumed his breast.

"Dog of the pale-faces!" he exclaimed, in Iroquois, "go yell among the curs of your own evil huntinggrounds!"

The denunciation was accompanied by an appropriate action. Even while speaking, his arm was lifted, and the tomahawk hurled. Luckily the loud tones of the speaker had drawn the eye of Deerslayer towards him, else would that moment have probably closed his career. So great was the dexterity with which this dangerous weapon was thrown, and so deadly the intent, that it would have riven the skull of the prisoner, had he not stretched forth an arm, and caught the handle in one of its turns, with a readiness quite as remarkable as the skill with which the missile had been hurled. The projectile force was so great, notwithstanding, that when Deerslayer's arm was arrested, his hand was raised above and behind his own head, and in the very attitude necessary to return the attack. It is not certain whether the circumstance of finding himself unexpectedly in this menacing posture and armed, tempted the young man to retaliate, or whether sudden resentment overcame his forbearance and prudence. His eye kindled, however, and a small red spot appeared on each cheek, while he cast all his energy in the effort of his arm, and threw back the weapon at his assailant. The unexpectedness of this blow contributed to its success, the Panther neither raising an arm nor bending his head to avoid it. The keen little axe struck the victim in a perpendicular line with the nose, directly between the eyes, literally braining him on the spot. Sallying forward, as the serpent darts at his enemy even while receiving its own death-wound, this man of powerful frame fell his length into the open area formed by the circle, quivering in death. A common rush to his relief left the captive, for a single instant, quite without the crowd, and, willing to make one desperate effort for life he bounded off with the activity of a deer. There was but a breathless instant, when the whole band, old and young, women and children, abandoning the lifeless body of the Panther where it lay, raised the yell of alarm, and followed in pursuit.

Sudden as had been the event which induced Deerslayer to make this desperate trial of speed, his mind was not wholly unprepared for the fearful emergency. In the course of the past hour, he had pondered well on the chances of such an experiment, and had shrewdly calculated all the details of success and failure. At the

first leap, therefore, his body was completely under the
direction of an intelligence that turned all its efforts to
the best account, and prevented everything like hesitation
or indecision, at the important instant of the start. To this
alone was he indebted for the first great advantage, that
of getting through the line of sentinels unharmed.

Several rifles were discharged at Deerslayer as he
came out into the comparative exposure of the clear
forest. But the direction of his line of flight, which partially crossed that of the fire, the haste with which the
weapons had been aimed, and the general confusion that
prevailed in the camp, prevented any harm from being
done. Bullets whistled past him, and many cut twigs from
the branches at his side, but not one touched even his
dress. The delay caused by these fruitless attempts was of
great service to the fugitive, who had gained more than
a hundred yards on even the leading men of the Hurons,
ere something like concert and order had entered into
the chase. To think of following with rifle in hand was
out of the question; and after emptying their pieces in
vague hopes of wounding their captive, the best runners
of the Indians threw them aside, calling out to the women
and boys to recover and load them again as soon as
possible.

Deerslayer knew too well the desperate nature of
the struggle in which he was engaged, to lose one of the
precious moments. He also knew that his only hope was
to run in a straight line, for as soon as he began to turn,
or double, the greater number of his pursuers would put
escape out of the question. He held his way, therefore,
in a diagonal direction up the acclivity, which was neither
very high nor very steep in this part of the mountain, but
which was sufficiently toilsome for one contending for
life, to render it painfully oppressive. There, however,
he slackened his speed to recover his breath, proceeding
even at a quick walk or a slow trot, along the more difficult parts of the way. The Hurons were whooping and
leaping behind him; but this he disregarded, well knowing they must overcome the difficulties he had sur-

mounted ere they could reach the elevation to which he had attained. The summit of the first hill was not quite near him, and he saw, by the formation of the land, that a deep glen intervened, before the base of a second hill could be reached. Walking deliberately to the summit, he glanced eagerly about him in every direction, in quest of a cover. None offered in the ground; but a fallen tree lay near him, and desperate circumstances require desperate remedies. This tree lay in a line parallel to the glen, at the brow of the hill; to leap on it, and then to force his person as close as possible under its lower side, took but a moment. Previously to disappearing from his pursuers, however, Deerslayer stood on the height and gave a cry of triumph, as if exulting at the sight of the descent that lay before him.—In the next instant he was stretched beneath the tree.

No sooner was this expedient adopted, than the young man ascertained how desperate had been his own efforts, by the violence of the pulsations in his frame. He could hear his heart beat, and his breathing was like the action of a bellows in quick motion. Breath was gained, however, and the heart soon ceased to throb as if about to break through its confinement. The footsteps of those who toiled up the opposite side of the acclivity were now audible, and presently voices and treads announced the arrival of the pursuers. The foremost shouted as they reached the favor of the descent, each leaped upon the fallen tree, height; then, fearful that their enemy would escape under and plunged into the ravine, trusting to get a sight of the pursued ere he reached the bottom. In this manner, Huron followed Huron, until Natty began to hope the whole had passed. Others succeeded, however, until quite forty had leaped over the tree; and then he counted them, as the surest mode of ascertaining how many could be behind. Presently all were in the bottom of the glen, quite a hundred feet below him, and some had even ascended part of the opposite hill, when it became evident an inquiry was making as to the direction he had taken. This was the critical moment; and one of nerves less steady, or of a training that had been neglected, would have seized it to rise, and fly. Not so with Deerslayer. He still lay quiet, watching with jealous vigilance every movement below, and fast regaining his breath.

The Hurons now resembled a pack of hounds at fault. Little was said, but each man ran about, examining the dead leaves, as the hound hunts for the lost scent. The great number of moccasins that had passed made the examination difficult, though the in-toe of an Indian was easily to be distinguished from the freer and wider step of a white man. Believing that no more pursuers remained behind, and hoping to steal away unseen, Deerslayer suddenly threw himself over the tree, and fell on the upper side. This achievement appeared to be effected successfully, and hope beat high in the bosom of the fugitive. Rising to his hands and feet, after a moment lost in listening to the sounds in the glen, in order to ascertain if he had been seen, the young man next scrambled to the top of the hill, a distance of only ten yards, in the expectation of getting its brow between him and his pursuers, and himself so far under cover. Even this was effected, and he rose to his feet, walking swiftly but steadily along the summit, in a direction opposite to that in which he had first fled.

Questions

1. The location of the meeting was:

   a. on the shore of a forest stream
   b. on the buffalo prairie
   c. in a clearing canopied by leaves
   d. in a teepee

2. The talents of the two chiefs were respectively:

   a. wisdom/bravery
   b. swiftness of foot/animal cunning
   c. eloquence/intelligence
   d. impassing height/distinguished as a warrior

3. Deerslayer's dialect was:

   a. Erie
   b. Iroquois
   c. Huron `
   d. Delaware

4. The repercussions of Deerslayer's guilty act included:

   a. a proposition to replace the dead man in the family and village
   b. leaving a widow and many fatherless children without food
   c. a long suspenseful wait for the council verdict
   d. all of the above

5. Deerslayer rejected the request to join the tribe because:

   a. Sumach was old and ugly
   b. he was not a good hunter
   c. he was afraid for his safety
   d. he couldn't marry a heathen Indian

6. The chief responded with:

   a. an arrow
   b. a carefully thrown tomahawk
   c. a carefully thrown spear
   d. pleas for Deerslayer to reconsider

7. Deerslayer escaped when:

   a. the council met to make a new proposal
   b. everyone rushed to the aid of the dying chief
   c. Sumach spit on him
   d. none of the above

8. His escape was successful because:

   a. he ran in a straight line
   b. he had pre-planned his course
   c. he hid under a fallen tree
   d. all of the above

9. The Indians' weapons included:

   a. bow and arrows
   b. rifles

    c. poison darts

    d. hunting hounds

10. The chase became confused because:

    a. the descent had made Deerslayer's escape hard

    b. there were too many Indians to maintain order

    c. the Indians had no way of crossing the river

    d. the Indians lost Deerslayer's trail

Answers

1.	c	6.	b
2.	a	7.	b
3.	d	8.	d
4.	d	9.	b
5.	d	10.	d

Spiral

    The next movement will be a welcome change for it is the most natural of the pacing movements and therefore easiest to do. Simply pace across the line, turning down at the end of the line, making a return sweep that brings you back up under the next line you wish to read (Fig. 4-3).

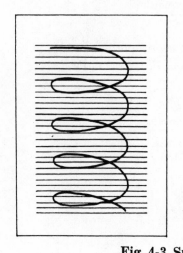 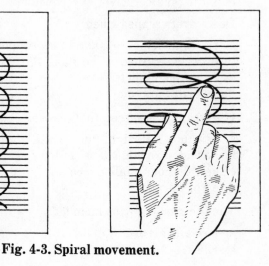

Fig. 4-3. Spiral movement.

Practice this "Spiral pacing motion" for several minutes in your novel. When you feel ready, practice it on the following article. Time yourself for five minutes so you can compare your rate for the Spiral with other movements.

Fenimore Cooper's Literary Offenses
by Samuel L. Clemens

The Pathfinder and The Deerslayer stand at the head of Cooper's novels as artistic creations. There are others of his works which contain parts as perfect as are to be found in these, and scenes even more thrilling. Not one can be compared with either of them as a finished whole.

The defects in both of these tales are comparatively slight. They were pure works of art.

PROF. LOUNSBURY

The five tales reveal an extraordinary fullness of invention. . . . One of the very greatest characters in fiction, Natty Bumppo. . . . The craft of the woodsman, the trick of the trapper, all the delicate art of the forest, were familiar to Cooper from his youth up.

PROF. BRANDER MATTHEWS

Cooper is the greatest artist in the domain of romantic fiction yet produced by America.

WILKIE COLLINS

It seems to me that it was far from right for the Professor of English Literature in Yale, the Professor of English Literature in Columbia, and Wilkie Collins to deliver opinions on Cooper's literature without having read some of it. It would have been much more decorous to keep silent and let persons talk who have read Cooper.

Cooper's art has some defects. In one place in *Deerslayer,* and in the restricted space of two-thirds of a page, Cooper has scored 114 offenses against literary art out of a possible 115. It breaks the record.

There are nineteen rules governing literary art in the domain of romantic fiction—some say twenty-two. In *Deerslayer,* Cooper violated eighteen of them. These eighteen require:

1. That a tale shall accomplish something and arrive somewhere. But the *Deerslayer* tale accomplishes nothing and arrives in the air.

2. They require that the episodes of a tale shall be necessary parts of the tale, and shall help to develop it. But as the *Deerslayer* tale is not a tale, and accomplishes nothing and arrives nowhere, the episodes have no rightful place in the work, since there was nothing for them to develop.

3. They require that the personages in a tale shall be alive, except in the case of corpses, and that always the reader shall be able to tell the corpses from the others. But this detail has often been overlooked in the *Deerslayer* tale.

4. They require that the personages in a tale, both dead and alive, shall exhibit a sufficient excuse for being there. But this detail also has been overlooked in the *Deerslayer* tale.

5. They require that when the personages of a tale deal in conversation, the talk shall sound like human talk, and be talk such as human beings would be likely to talk in the given circumstances, and have a discoverable meaning, also a discoverable purpose, and a show of relevancy, and remain in the neighborhood of the subject in hand, and be interesting to the reader, and help out the tale, and stop when the people cannot think of anything more to say. But this requirement has been ignored from the beginning of the *Deerslayer* tale to the end of it.

6. They require that when the author describes the character of a personage in his tale, the conduct and conversation of that personage shall justify said description. But this law gets little or no attention in the *Deerslayer* tale, as Natty Bumppo's case will amply prove.

7. They require that when a personage talks like an illustrated gilt-edged, tree-calf, hand-tooled, seven-dollar Friendship's Offering in the beginning of a paragraph he shall not talk like a negro minstrel in the end of it. But this rule is flung down and danced upon in the *Deerslayer*.

8. They require that crass stupidities shall not be played upon the reader as "the craft of the woodsman, the delicate art of the forest," by either the author or the people in the tale. But this rule is persistently violated in the *Deerslayer* tale.

9. They require that the personages of a tale shall confine themselves to possibilities and let miracles alone; or if they venture a miracle, the author must so plausibly set it forth as to make it look possible and reasonable. But these rules are not respected in the *Deerslayer* tale.

10. They require that the author shall make the reader feel a deep interest in the personages of his tale and in their fate; and that he shall make the reader love the good people in the tale and hate the bad ones. But the reader of the *Deerslayer* tale dislikes the good people in it, is indifferent to the others, and wishes they would all get drowned together.

11. They require that the characters in a tale shall be so clearly defined that the reader can tell beforehand what each will do in a given emergency. But in the *Deerslayer* this rule is vacated.

In addition to these large rules there are some little ones. These require that the author shall:

12. Say what he is proposing to say, not merely come near it.

13. Use the right word, not its second cousin.

14. Eschew surplusage.

15. Not omit necessary details.

16. Avoid slovenliness of form.

17. Use good grammar.

18. Employ a simple and straightforward style.

Even these seven are coldly and persistently violated in the *Deerslayer* tale.

Cooper's gift in the way of invention was not a rich endowment; but such as it was he liked to work it; he was pleased with the effects, and indeed he did some quite sweet things with it. In his little box of stage-properties he kept six or eight cunning devices, tricks, artifices for his savages and woodsmen to deceive and circumvent each other with, and he was never so happy as when he was working these innocent things and seeing them go. A favorite one was to make a moccasined person tread in the tracks of the moccasined enemy, and thus hide his own trail. Cooper wore out barrels and barrels of moccasins in working that trick. Another stage-property that he pulled out of his box pretty frequently was his broken twig. He prized his broken twig above all the rest of his effects, and worked it the hardest. It is a restful chapter in any book of his when somebody doesn't step on a dry twig and alarm all the reds and whites for two hundred yards around. Every time a Cooper person is in peril, and absolute silence is worth four dollars a minute, he is sure to step on a dry twig. There may be a hundred handier things to step on, but that wouldn't satisfy Cooper. Cooper requires him to turn out and find a dry twig; and if he can't do it, go and borrow one. In fact, the Leatherstocking series ought to have been called the Broken Twig Series.

I am sorry there is not room to put in a few dozen instances of the delicate art of the forest, as practiced by Natty Bumppo and some of the other Cooperian experts. Perhaps we may venture two or three samples. Cooper was a sailor—a naval officer; yet he gravely tells us how a vessel, driving toward a lee shore in a gale, is steered for a particular spot by her skipper because he knows of an *undertow* there which will hold her back against the gale and save her. For just pure woodcraft, or sailorcraft, or whatever it is, isn't that neat? For several years Cooper was daily in the society of artillery, and he ought to have noticed that when a cannon-ball strikes the ground it either buries itself or skips a hundred feet or so; skips again a hundred feet or so— and so on, till finally it gets tired and rolls. Now in one place he loses some "females"—as he always calls women—in the edge of a wood near a plain at night in a fog, on purpose to give Bumppo a chance to show off the delicate art of the forest before the reader. These mislaid people are hunting for a fort. They hear a cannon-blast, and a cannon-ball presently comes rolling into the wood and stops at their feet. To the females this suggests nothing. The case is very different with the admirable Bumppo. I wish I may never know peace again if he doesn't strike out promptly and *follow the track* of that cannon-ball across the plain through the dense fog and find the fort. Isn't it a daisy? If Cooper had any real knowledge of Nature's way of doing things, he had a most delicate art in concealing the fact. For instance: one of his acute Indian experts, Chingachgook (pronounced Chicago, I think), has lost the trail of a person he is tracking through the forest. Apparently that trail is hopelessly lost. Neither you nor I could ever have guessed out the way to find it. It was very different with Chicago. Chicago was not stumped for long. He turned a running stream out of its course and there in the slush of its old bed, were that person's moccasin tracks. The current did not wash them away, as it would have done in all other like cases—no, even the eternal laws of Nature have to vacate when Cooper wants to put up a delicate job of woodcraft on the reader.

We must be a little wary when Brander Matthews tells us that Cooper's books "reveal an extraordinary fullness of invention." As a rule, I am quite willing to accept Brander Matthews' literary judgments and applaud his lucid and graceful phrasing of them; but that particular statement needs to be taken with a few tons of salt. Bless your heart, Cooper hasn't any more invention than a horse; and I don't mean a high-class horse, either; I mean a clotheshorse. It would be very difficult to find a really clever "situation" in Cooper's books, and still more difficult to find one of any kind which he has failed to render absurd by his handling of it. Look at the episodes of "the caves"; and at the celebrated scuffle between Maqua and those others on the tableland a few days later; and at Hurry Harry's queer water-transit from the castle to the ark; and at Deerslayer's half-hour with his first corpse; and at the quarrel between Hurry Harry and Deerslayer later; and at—but choose for yourself.

If Cooper had been an observer his inventive faculty would have worked better; not more interestingly, but more rationally, more plausibly. Cooper's proudest creations in the way of "situations" suffer noticeably from the absence of the observer's protecting gift. Cooper's eye was splendidly inaccurate. Cooper seldom saw anything correctly. He saw nearly all things as through a glass eye, darkly. Of course a man who cannot see the commonest little everyday matters accurately is working at a disadvantage when he is constructing a "situation." In the *Deerslayer* tale Cooper has a stream which is fifty feet wide where it flows out of a lake; it presently narrows to twenty as it meanders along for no given reason, and yet when a stream acts like that it ought to be required to explain itself. Fourteen pages later the width of the brook's outlet from the lake has suddenly shrunk thirty feet, and became "the narrowest part of the stream." This shrinkage is not accounted for. The stream has bends in it, a sure indication that has alluvial banks and cuts them; yet these bends are only thirty and fifty feet long. If Cooper had been a nice and punctilious observer he would have noticed that the bends were oftener nine hundred feet long than short of it.

Cooper made the exit of that stream fifty feet wide, in the first place, for no particular reason; in the second place, he narrowed it to less than twenty to accommodate some Indians. He bends a "sapling" to the form of an arch over this narrow passage, and conceals six Indians in its foliage. They are "laying" for a settler's scow or ark which is coming up the stream on its way to the lake; it is being hauled against the stiff current by a rope whose stationary end is anchored in the lake; its rate of progress cannot be more than a mile an hour. Cooper describes the ark, but pretty obscurely. In the matter of dimensions "It was little more than a modern canal-boat." Let us guess, then, that it was about one hundred and forty feet long. It was of "greater breadth than common." Let us guess, then, that it was about sixteen feet wide. This leviathan has been prowling down bends which were but a third as long as itself, and scraping between where it had only two feet of space to spare on each side. We can not too much admire this miracle. A low-roofed log dwelling occupies "two-thirds of the ark's length"—a dwelling ninety feet long and sixteen feet wide, let us say—a kind of vestibule train. The dwelling has two rooms—each forty-five feet long and sixteen feet wide, let us guess. One of them is the bedroom of the Hutter girls, Judith and Hetty; the other is the parlor in the day time, at night it is papa's bedchamber. The ark is arriving at the stream's exit now, whose width has been reduced to less than twenty feet to accommodate the Indians— say to eighteen. There is a foot to spare on each side of the boat. Did the Indians notice that there was going to be a tight squeeze there? Did they notice that they could make money, by climbing down out of that arched sapling and just stepping aboard when the ark scraped by? No, other Indians would have noticed these things, but Cooper's Indians never noticed anything. Cooper thinks they are marvelous creatures for noticing but he was almost always in error about his Indians. There was seldom a sane one among them.

The ark is one hundred and forty feet long; the dwelling is ninety feet long. The idea of the Indians is to drop softly and secretly from the arched sapling to the dwelling as the ark creeps along under it at the rate of a mile an hour, and butcher the family. It will take the ark a minute and a half to pass under. It will take the ninety-foot dwelling a minute to pass under. Now, then, what did the six Indians do? It would take you thirty years to guess, and even then you would have to give it up, I believe. Therefore, I will tell you what the Indians did. Their chief, a person of quite extraordinary intellect for a Cooper Indian, warily watched the canal-boat as it squeezed along under him, and when he had got his calculations fined down to exactly the right shade, as he judged, he let go and dropped. And missed the house! That is actually what he did. He missed the house, and landed in the stern of the scow. It was not much of a fall, yet it knocked him silly. He lay there unconscious. If the house had been ninety-seven feet long he would have made the trip. The fault was Cooper's, not his. The error lay in the construction of the house. Cooper was no architect.

There still remained in the roost five Indians. The boat has passed under and is now out of their reach. Let me explain what the five did—you would not be able to reason it out for yourself. No. 1 jumped for the boat, but fell in the water astern of it. Then No. 2 jumped for the boat, but fell in the water still farther astern of it. Then No. 3 jumped for the boat, and fell a good way astern of it. Then No. 4 jumped for the boat, and fell in the water away stern. Then even No. 5 made a jump for the boat— for he was a Cooper Indian. In the matter of intellect, the difference between a Cooper Indian and the Indian that stands in front of the cigar-shop is not spacious. The scow episode is really a sublime burst of invention; but it does not thrill, because the inaccuracy of the details throws a sort of air of fictitiousness and general improbability over it. This comes of Cooper's inadequacies as an observer.

The reader will find some examples of Cooper's high talent for inaccurate observation in the account of the shooting-match in *The Pathfinder*.

A common wrought nail was driven lightly into the target, its head having first touched with paint.

The color of the paint is not stated—an important omission, but Cooper deals freely in important omissions. No, after all, it was not an important omission; for this nail-head is a *hundred yards* from the marksmen, and could not be seen by them at that distance, no matter what its color might be. How far can the best eyes see a common house-fly? A hundred yards? It is quite impossible. Very well: eyes that cannot see a house-fly that is a hundred yards away cannot see an ordinary nail-head at that distance, for the size of the two objects is the same. It takes a keen eye to see a fly or a nailhead at fifty yards, one hundred and fifty feet. Can the reader do it?

The nail was lightly driven, its head painted, and game called. Then the Cooper miracles began. The bullet of the first marksman chipped an edge of the nail-head; the next man's bullet drove the nail a little way into the target—and removed all the paint. Haven't the miracles gone far enough now? Not to suit Cooper; for the purpose of this whole scheme is to show off his prodigy, Deer-slayer-Hawkeye-Long-Rifle-Leatherstocking-Pathfinder-Bumppo before the ladies.

"Be all ready to clench it, boys!" cried out Pathfinder, stepping into his friend's tracks the instant they were vacant. "Never mind a new nail; I can see that, though the paint is gone, and what I can see I can hit at a hundred yards, though it were only a mosquito's eye. Be ready to clench!"

The rifle cracked, the bullet sped its way, and the head of the nail was buried in the wood, covered by the piece of flattened lead.

There, you see, is a man who could hunt flies with a rifle, and command a ducal salary in a Wild West show today if we had him back with us.

The recorded feat is certainly surprising just as it stands; but it is not surprising enough for Cooper. Cooper adds a touch. He has made Pathfinder do this miracle with another man's rifle; and not only that, but Pathfinder did not have even the advantage of loading it himself. He had everything against him, and yet he made that impossible shot; and not only made it, but did it with absolute confidence, saying, "Be ready to clench." Now a person like that would have undertaken that same feat with a brickbat, and with Cooper to help he would have achieved it, too.

Pathfinder shows off handsomely that day before the ladies. His very first feat was a thing which no Wild West show can touch. He was standing with the group of marksmen, observing—a hundred yards from the target, mind; one Jasper raised his rifle and drove the center of the bull's-eye. Then the Quartermaster fired. The target exhibited no result this time. There was a laugh. "It's a dead miss." said Major Lundie. Pathfinder waited an impressive moment or two; then said, in that calm, indifferent, know-it-all way of his, "No, Major, he has covered Jasper's bullet, as will be seen if anyone will take the trouble to examine the target.

Wasn't it remarkable? How *could* he see that little pellet fly through the air and enter that distant bullet-hole? Yet that is what he did; for nothing is impossible to a Cooper person. Did any of those people have any deep-seated doubts about this thing? No, for that would imply sanity, and these were all Cooper people.

The respect for Pathfinder's skill and for his *quickness and accuracy of sight* [italics are mine] was so profound and general, that the instant he made this declaration the spectators began to distrust their own opinions, and a dozen rushed to the target in order to ascertain the fact. There, sure enough, it was found that the Quartermaster's bullet had gone through the hole made by Jasper's, and that, too, so accurately as to require a minute examination to be certain of the circumstance, which, however, was soon clearly established by discovering one bullet over the other in the stump against which the target was placed.

They made a "minute" examination; but never mind, how could they know that there were two bullets in that hole without digging the latest one out? for neither probe nor eyesight could prove the presence of any more than one bullet. Did they dig? No; as we shall see. It is the Pathfinder's turn now; he steps out before the ladies, takes aim, and fires.

But alas! here is a disappointment; an incredible, an unimaginable disappointment—for the target's aspect is unchanged; there is nothing there but that same old bullet-hole!

"If one dared to hint at such a thing," cried Major Duncan, "I should say that Pathfinder has also missed the target!"

As nobody had missed it yet, the "also" was not necessary; but never mind about that, for the Pathfinder is going to speak.

"No, no, Major," said he, confidently, "that would be a risky declaration. I didn't load the piece, and can't say what was in it; but if it was lead, you will find the bullet driving down those of the Quartermaster and Jasper, else is not my name Pathfinder."

A shout from the target announced the truth of this assertion.

Is the miracle sufficient as it stands? Not for Cooper. The Pathfinder speaks again, as he "now slowly advances toward the stage occupied by the females":

> "That's not all, boys, that's not all; if you find the target touched at all, I'll own to a miss. The Quartermaster cut the wood, but you'll find no wood cut by that last messenger."

The miracle is at last complete. He knew—doubtless saw—at the distance of a hundred yards—that his bullet had passed into the hole *without fraying the edges*. There were now three bullets in that one hole—three bullets embedded processionally in the body of the stump back of the target. Everybody knew this—somehow or other—and yet nobody had dug any of them out to make sure. Cooper is not a close observer, but he is interesting. He is certainly always that, no matter what happens. And he is more interesting when he is not noticing what he is about than when he is. This is a considerable merit.

The conversations in the Cooper books have a curious sound in our modern ears. To believe that such talk really ever came out of people's mouths would be to believe that there was a time when time was of no value to a person who thought he had something to say; when it was the custom to spread a two-minute remark out to ten; when a man's mouth was a rolling-mill, and busied itself all day long in turning four-foot pigs of thought into thirty-foot bars of conversational railroad iron by attenuation; when subjects were seldom faithfully stuck to, but the talk wandered all around and arrived nowhere; when conversations consisted mainly of irrelevancies, with here and there a relevancy, a relevancy with an embarrassed look, a not being able to explain how it got there.

Cooper was certainly not a master in the construction of dialogue. Inaccurate observation defeated him here as it defeated him in so many other enterprises of his. He even failed to notice that the man who talks corrupt English six days in a week must and will talk it on the seventh, and can't help himself. In the *Deerslayer* story he lets Deerslayer talk the showiest kind of book-talk sometimes, and at other times the basest of base dialects. For instance, when some one asks him if he has a sweetheart, and if so, where she abides, this is his majestic answer:

"She's in the forest—hanging from the boughs of the trees, in a soft rain on the dew on the open grass—the clouds that float about in the blue heaven—the birds that sing in the woods—the sweet springs where I slake my thirst—and in all the other glorious gifts that come from God's Providence!"

And he preceded that, a little before, with this:

"It consarns me as all things that touches a fri'nd consarns a fri'nd."

And this another of his remarks:

"If I was Injun born, now, I might tell of this, or carry in the scalp and boast of the explite afore the whole tribe; or if my inimy had only been a bear"—[and so on].

We cannot imagine such a thing as a veteran Scotch Commander-in-Chief comporting himself in the field like a windy melodramatic actor, but Cooper could. On one occasion Alice and Cora were being chased by the French through a fog in the neighborhood of their father's fort:

"Point de quartier aux coquins!" cried an eager pursuer, who seemed to direct the operations of the enemy.
"Stand firm and be ready, my gallant 60ths!" suddenly exclaimed a voice above them; "wait to see the enemy; fire low, and sweep the glacis."
"Father! father!" exclaimed a piercing cry from out the mist; "it is I! Alice! thy own Elsie! spare, O! save your daughters!"
"Hold" shouted the former speaker, in the awful tones of parental agony, the sound reaching even to the woods, and rolling back in solemn echo. "Tis she! God has restored me my children! Throw open the sallyports to the field, 60ths, to the field! pull not a trigger, lest ye kill my lambs! Drive off these dogs of France with your steel!"

Cooper's word-sense was singularly dull. When a person has poor ear for music he will flat and sharp right along without knowing it. He keeps near the tune, but it is *not* the tune. When a person has a poor ear for words, the result is literary flatting and sharping; you perceive what he is intending to say, but you also perceive that he doesn't *say* it. This is Cooper. He was not a word-musician. His ear was satisfied with the *approximate* word. I will furnish some circumstantial evidence in support of this charge. My instances are gathered from half a dozen pages of the tale called *Deerslayer*. He uses "verbal" for "oral"; "precision" for "facility"; "phenomena" for "marvels"; "necessary" for "predetermined"; "unsophisticated" for "primitive"; "preparation" for "expectancy"; "rebuked" for "subdued"; "dependent on" for "resulting from"; "fact" for "condition"; "fact" for "conjecture"; "precaution" for "caution"; explanation" for "determine"; "mortified" for "disappointed"; "meretricious" for "factitious"; "materially" for "considerably"; "decreasing" for "deepening"; "increasing" for "disappearing"; "embedded" for "enclosed"; "treacherous" for "hostile"; "stood" for "stooped"; "rejoined" for remarked"; "situation" for "condition"; "different" for "differing"; "brevity" for "celerity"; "distrusted" for "suspicious"; "mental imbecility" for "imbecility"; "eyes" for "sight"; "counteracting" for "opposing"; "funeral obsequies" for "obsequies."

There have been daring people in the world who claimed that Cooper could write English, but they are all dead now—all dead but Lounsbury. I don't remember that Lounsbury makes the claim in so many words, still he makes it, for he says the *Deerslayer* is a "pure work of art." Pure, in that connection, means faultless— faultless in all details—and language is a detail. If Mr. Lounsbury had only compared Cooper's English with the English which he writes himself—but it is plain that he didn't; and so it is likely that he imagines until this day that Cooper's is as clear and compact as his own. Now I feel sure, deep down in my heart, that Cooper wrote about the poorest English that exists in our language, and that the English of *Deerslayer* is the very worst that even Cooper ever wrote.

I may be mistaken, but it does seem to me that *Deerslayer* is just simply a literary *delirium tremens*.

A work of art? It has no invention; it has no order, system, sequence, or result; it has no life-likeness, no thrill, no stir, no seeming of reality; its characters are confusedly drawn, and by their acts and words they prove that they are not the sort of people the author claims that they are; its humor is pathetic; its pathos is funny; its conversations are—oh! indescribable; its love scenes odious; its English a crime against the language.

Counting these out what is left is Art. I think we must all admit that.

Questions

1. Clemens feels that the three opinions at the beginning of this article are offered by men:

   a. who are qualified to speak on the subject
   b. who had never read some of Cooper's literature
   c. who are anti-Cooper
   d. who are not qualified to speak

2. According to Clemens, Cooper scored 114 offenses against literary art in the space of:

   a. one chapter
   b. two-thirds of a chapter
   c. two-thirds of a page
   d. two-thirds of the book

3. Eighteen of the _____rules governing literary art in the domain of romantic fiction are quoted.

   a. 19
   b. 25
   c. 115
   d. 30

4. The tale being evaluated according to the eighteen rules is:

   a. The Pathfinder
   b. The Deerslayer
   c. The Last of the Mohicans

5. Because of the repeated use of this "stage prop," Clemens suggests that the Leatherstocking series ought to have been called:

   a. The Cannon-ball series
   b. The Broken Twig series
   c. The woodcraft series

6. Cooper's profession was:

   a. sailor
   b. architect
   c. builder
   d. woodsman

7. Cooper has a high talent for:

   a. exaggeration
   b. inaccurate observation
   c. description
   d. metaphor

8. According to the author, the most remarkable thing about Pathfinder is:

   a. his shooting ability
   b. his fame with the ladies
   c. his unusually keen eyesight

9. Cooper's word-sense is compared to that of:

   a. a poet
   b. someone with no ear for music
   c. a great spokesman
   d. a melodramatic actor

10. According to Clemens, Cooper wrote:

    a. about the poorest English that exists in our language
    b. fantastic dialogue
    c. realistically
    d. a pure work of art

Answers

1. b   6. a

2.	c	7.	b
3.	a	8.	c
4.	b	9.	b
5.	b	10.	a

Hop

You are now ready to learn your last pacing motion, the *Hop*. It is particularly effective because it emphasizes seeing

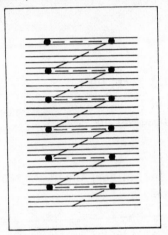

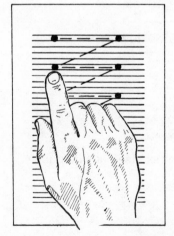

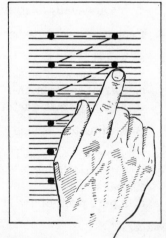

Fig. 4-4. Hop movement.

groups of words at one fixation, rather than seeing individual words, is rhythmical and very fast. In this movement, instead of sliding your finger under each line, you are to *point at each half of the line.* As you read, this pointing quickly takes on a hopping motion as you raise and lower your eyes on each group of words. If you find that you are missing some words with two jumps per line, you may wish to practice the motion by hopping three times per line. After you *hop* around in your next reading selection, take a five-minute reading drill in your novel using the Hop. If you haven't entered your rate from the last drill on your record sheet, do so now.

The Town Dump
by Wallace Stegner

The town dump of Whitemud, Saskatchewan, could only have been a few years old when I knew it, for the village was born in 1913 and I left there in 1919. But I remember the dump better than I remember most things in that town, better than I remember most of the people. I spent more time with it, for one thing; it has more poetry and excitement in it than people did.

It lay in the southeast corner of town, in a section that was always full of adventure for me. Just there the Whitemud River left the hills, bent a little south, and started its long traverse across the prairie and international boundary to join the Milk. For all I knew, it might have been on its way to join the Alph: simply, before my eyes, it disappeared into strangeness and wonder.

Also, where it passed below the dumpground, it ran through willowed bottoms that were a favorite campsite for passing teamsters, gypsies, sometimes Indians. The very straw scattered around those camps, the ashes of those strangers' campfires, the manure of their teams and saddle horses, were hot with adventurous possibilities.

It was as an extension, a living suburb, as it were, of the dumpground that we most valued those camps. We scoured them for artifacts of their migrant tenants as if they had been archaeological sites full of the secrets of ancient civilizations. I remember toting around for weeks the broken cheek strap of a bridle. Somehow or other its buckle looked as if it had been fashioned in a far place, a place where they were accustomed to flatten the tongues of buckles for reasons that could only be exciting, and where they made a habit of plating the metal with some valuable alloy, probably silver. In places where the silver was worn away the buckle underneath shone dull yellow: probably gold.

It seemed that excitement liked that end of town better than our end. Once old Mrs. Gustafson, deeply religious and a little raddled in the head, went over there with a buckboard full of trash, and as she was driving home along the river she looked and saw a spent catfish, washed in from Cypress Lake or some other part of the watershed, floating on the yellow water. He was two feet long, his whiskers hung down, his fins and tail were limp. He was a kind of fish that no one had seen in the Whitemud in the three or four years of the town's life, and a kind that none of us children had ever seen anywhere. Mrs. Gustafson had never seen one like him either; she perceived at once that he was the devil, and she whipped up the team and reported him at Hoffman's elevator.

We could hear her screeching as we legged it for the river to see for ourselves. Sure enough, there he was. He looked very tired, and he made no great effort to get away as we pushed out a half-sunken rowboat below the flume, submerged it under him, and brought him ashore. When he died three days later we experimentally fed him to two half-wild cats, but they seemed to suffer no ill effects.

At that same end of town the irrigation flume crossed the river. It always seemed to me giddily high when I hung my chin over its plank edge and looked down, but it probably walked no more than twenty feet above the water on its spidery legs. Ordinarily in summer it carried about six or eight inches of smooth water, and under the glassy hurrying of the little boxed stream the planks were coated with deep sun-warmed moss as slick as frogs' eggs. A boy could sit in the flume of water walling up against his back, and grab a cross brace above him, and pull, shooting himself sledlike ahead until he could reach the next brace for another pull and another slide, and so on across the river in four scoots.

After ten minutes in the flume he would come out wearing a dozen or more limber black leeches, and could sit in the green shade where darning needles flashed blue, and dragonflies hummed and darted and stopped, and skaters dimpled slack and eddy with their delicate transitory footprints, and there stretch the leeches out one by one while their sucking ends clung and clung, until at last, stretched far out, they let go with a tiny wet puk and snapped together like rubber bands. The smell of the river and the flume and the clay cutbanks and the bars of that part of the river was the smell of wolf willow.

But nothing in that end of town was as good as the dumpground that scattered along a little runoff coulee dipping down toward the river from the south bench. Through a historical process that went back, probably, to the roots of community sanitation and distaste for eyesores, but that in law dated from the Unincorporated Towns Ordinance of the territorial government, passed in 1888, the dump was one of the very first community enterprises, almost our town's first institution.

More than that, it contained relics of every individual who had ever lived there, and of every phase of the town's history.

The bedsprings on which the town's first child was begotten might be there; the skeleton of a boy's pet colt; two or three volumes of Shakespeare bought in haste and error from a peddler, later loaned in carelessness, soaked with water and chemicals in a house fire, and finally thrown out to flap their stained eloquence in the prairie wind.

Broken dishes, rusty tinware, spoons that had been used to mix paint; once a box of percussion caps, sign and

symbol of the carelessness that most of those people felt
about all matters of personal or public safety. We put
them on the railroad tracks and were anonymously de-
nounced in the *Enterprise*. There were also old iron, old
brass, for which we hunted assiduously, by night conning
junkmen's catalogues and the pages of the *Enterprise* to
find how much wartime value there might be in the
geared insides of clocks or in a pound of tea lead carefully wrapped in a ball whose weight astonished and
delighted us. Sometimes the unimaginable outside world
reached in and laid a finger on us. I recall that, aged no
more than seven, I wrote a St. Louis junk house asking
if they preferred their tea lead and tinfoil wrapped in
balls, or whether they would rather have it pressed flat in
sheets, and I got back a typewritten letter in a window
envelope instructing me that they would be happy to have
it in any way that was convenient for me. They added
that they valued my business and were mine very truly.
Dazed, I carried that windowed grandeur around in my
pocket until I wore it out, and for months I saved the
letter as a souvenir of the wondering time when something strange and distinguished had singled me out.

We hunted old bottles in the dump, bottles caked with
dirt and filth, half buried, full of cobwebs, and we washed
them out at the horse trough by the elevator, putting in
a handfull of shot along with the water to knock the dirt
loose; and when we had shaken them until our arms were
tired, we hauled them off in somebody's coaster wagon
and turned them in at Bill Anderson's pool hall, where
the smell of lemon pop was so sweet on the dark pool-hall
air that I am sometimes awakened by it in the night,
even yet.

Smashed wheels of wagons and buggies, tangles of
rusty barbed wire, the collapsed perambulator that the
French wife of one of the town's doctors had once pushed
proudly up the planked side-walks and along the ditch-
bank paths. A welter of foul-smelling feathers and coyote-
scattered carrion which was all that remained of somebody's dream of a chicken ranch. The chickens had all

got some mysterious pip at the same time, and died as one, and the dream lay out there with the rest of the town's history to rustle to the empty sky on the border of the hills.

There was melted glass in curious forms, and the half-melted office safe left from the burning of Bill Day's Hotel. On very lucky days we might find a piece of the lead casing that had enclosed the wires of the town's first telephone system. The casing was just the right size for rings, and so soft that it could be whittled with a jackknife. It was a material that might have made artists of us. If we had been Indians of fifty years before, that bright soft metal could have enlisted our maximum patience and craft and come out as ring and metal and amulet inscribed with the symbols of our observed world. Perhaps there were too many ready-made alternatives in the local drug, hardware, and general stores; perhaps our feeble artistic response was a measure of the insufficiency of the challenge we felt. In any case I do not remember that we did any more with the metal than to shape it into crude seal rings with our initials or pierced hearts carved in them; and these, though they served a purpose in juvenile courtship, stopped something short of art.

The dump held very little wood, for in that country anything burnable got burned. But it had plenty of old iron, furniture, papers, mattresses that were the delight of field mice, and jugs and demijohns that were sometimes their bane, for they crawled into the necks and drowned in the rainwater or redeye that was inside.

If the history of our town was not exactly written, it was at least hinted, in the dump. I think I had a pretty sound notion even at eight or nine of how significant was that first institution of our forming Canadian civilization. For rummaging through its foul purlieus I had several times been surprised and shocked to find relics of my own life tossed out there to rot or blow away.

The volumes of Shakespeare belonged to a set that my father had bought before I was born. It had been carried through successive moves from town to town in the Dakotas, and from Dakota to Seattle, and from Seattle to Bellingham, and Bellingham to Redmond, and from Redmond back to Iowa, and from there to Saskatchewan. Then, stained in a stranger's house fire, these volumes had suffered from a house-cleaning impulse and been thrown away for me to stumble upon in the dump. One of the Cratchet girls had borrowed them, a hatchet-faced, thin, eager, transplanted Cockney girl with a frenzy, almost a hysteria, for reading. And yet somehow, through her hands, they found the dump to become a symbol of how much was lost, how much thrown aside, how much carelessly or of necessity given up, in the making of a new country. We had so few books that I was familiar with them all, had handled them, looked at their pictures, perhaps even read them. They were the lares and penates, part of the skimpy impedimenta of household gods we had brought with us into Latium. Finding those three thrown away was like finding my name on a gravestone.

And yet not the blow that something else was, something that impressed me even more with the dump's close reflection of the town's intimate life. The colt whose picked skeleton lay out there was mine. He had been incurably crippled when dogs chased our mare, Daisy, the morning after she foaled. I had labored for months to make him well; had fed him by hand, curried him, exercised him, adjusted the iron braces that I had talked my father into having made. And I had not known that he would have to be destroyed. One weekend I turned him over to the foreman of one of the ranches, presumably so that he could be cared for. A few days later I found his skinned body, with the braces still on his crippled front legs, lying on the dump.

Not even that, I think, cured me of going there, though our parents all forbade us on pain of cholera or worse to do so. The place fascinated us, as it should have. For this was the kitchen midden of all the civilization we knew; it gave us the most tantalizing glimpses into our lives as well as into those of the neighbors. It gave us an aesthetic distance from which to know ourselves.

The dump was our poetry and our history. We took it home with us by the wagonload, bringing back into town the things the town had used and thrown away. Some little part of what we gathered, mainly bottles, we managed to bring back to usefulness, but most of our gleanings we left lying around barn or attic or cellar until in some renewed fury of spring cleanup our families carted them off to the dump again, to be rescued and briefly treasured by some other boy with schemes for making them useful. Occasionally something we really valued with a passion was snatched from us in horror and returned at once. That happened to the mounted head of a white mountain goat, somebody's trophy from old times and the far Rocky Mountains, that I brought home one day in transports of delight. My mother took one look and discovered that his beard was full of moths.

I remember that goat; I regret him yet. Poetry is seldom useful, but always memorable. I think I learned more from the town dump than I learned from school: more about people, more about how life is lived, not elsewhere but here, not in other times but now. If I were a sociologist anxious to study in detail the life of any community, I would go very early to its refuse piles. For a community may be as well judged by what it throws away—what it has thrown away and what it chooses to—as by any other evidence. For whole civilizations we have sometimes no more of the poetry and little more of the history than this.

Questions

1. The camps of migrant tents near the dump were likened to:

    a. an Indian village
    b. the ghetto
    c. archeological sites
    d. a wealthy suburb

2. The dump went through a historical process and was:

    a. declared unsanitary in 1881
    b. one of the first community institutions
    c. filled with black leeches
    d. where Mrs. Gustafson saw a catfish

3. The author once wrote a letter to a St. Louis junk house to:

    a. denounce some delinquents anonymously
    b. find the wartime value of clock gears
    c. find some matters of public safety
    d. see if they preferred their tinfoil wrapped in balls or pressed in sheets

4. The lead casing of the town's first telephone system was used for:

    a. making chains for prisoners
    b. making chicken wire fences
    c. melting into other forms of hardware
    d. rings with initials carved in them

5. The dump held very little:

    a. wood
    b. furniture
    c. papers
    d. mattresses

6. The author had been shocked to find in the dump:

    a. drowned field mice
    b. relics of his own life
    c. a collapsed perambulator
    d. a half-melted office safe

7. Finding his father's old volumes of Shakespeare was like finding:

    a. his own name on a gravestone
    b. a missing link from his past
    c. a precious jewel
    d. all of the above

8. The picked skeleton of a pony:

   a. had once belonged to the Crachet girl
   b. had lain there for fifty years
   c. had belonged to the author
   d. had once been a race horse

9. The dump was the town's:

   a. history
   b. poetry
   c. passion
   d. both a and b

10. A community may be judged by:

   a. its structure
   b. its people
   c. what it throws away
   d. its accomplishments

Answers

1.	c	6.	b
2.	b	7.	a
3.	d	8.	c
4.	d	9.	a
5.	a	10.	c

Things worth remembering are worth repeating. Since the Hop is a good pacing motion to remember and since most people find that it is the most efficient pacing movement, use it again, and on the next reading selection on the following pages.

Who Killed King Kong?
by X. J. Kennedy

The ordeal and spectacular death of King Kong, the giant ape, undoubtedly have been witnessed by more Americans than have ever seen a performance of *Hamlet, Iphigenia at Aulis,* or even *Tobacco Road.* Since RKO-Radio Pictures first released *King Kong,* a quarter-century has gone by; yet year after year, from prints that grow more rain-beaten, from sound tracks that grow more tinny, ticket-buyers by thousands still pursue Kong's luckless fight against the forces of technology, tabloid journalism, and the DAR. They have him chloroformed to sleep, see him whisked from his jungle home to New York and placed on show, see him burst his chains to scare the city (lugging a frightened blonde), at last to plunge from the spire of the Empire State Building machine-gunned by model airplanes.

Though Kong may die, one begins to think his legend unkillable. No clearer proof of his hold upon the popular imagination may be seen than what emerged one catastrophic week in March 1955, when New York WOR-TV programmed *Kong* for seven evenings in a row (a total of sixteen showings). Many a rival network vice-president must have scowled when surveys showed that *Kong* —the 1933 B-picture—had lured away fat segments of the viewing populace from such powerful competitors as Ed Sullivan, Groucho Marx and Bishop Sheen.

But even television has failed to run *King Kong* into oblivion. Coffee-in-the-lobby cinemas still show the old hunk of hokum, with the apology that in its use of composite shots and animated models the film remains technically interesting. And no other monster in movie history has won so devoted a popular audience. None of the plodding mummies, the stultified draculas, the white-coated Lugosis with their shiny pinball-machine laboratories, none of the invisible strangers, berserk robots, or menaces from Mars has ever enjoyed so many resurrections.

Why does the American public refuse to let King Kong rest in peace? It is true, I'll admit, that *Kong* outdid every monster movie before or since in sheer carnage. Producers Cooper and Schoedsack crammed into it dinosaurs, headhunters, riots, aerial battles, bullets, bombs, bloodletting. Heroine Fay Wray, whose function is mainly to scream, shuts her mouth for hardly one uninterrupted minute from first reel to last. It is also true that *Kong* is larded with good healthy sadism, for those whose joy it is to see the frantic girl dangled from cliffs and harried by pterodactyls. But it seems to me that the abiding appeal of the giant ape rests on other foundations.

Kong has, first of all, the attraction of being manlike. His simian nature gives him one huge advantage over giant ants and walking vegetables in that an audience many conceivably identify with him. Kong's appeal has the quality that established the Tarzan series as American myth—for what man doesn't secretly image himself a huge hairy howler against whom no other monster has a chance? If Tarzan recalls the ape in us, then Kong may well appeal to that great-granddaddy primordial brute from whose tribe we have all deteriorated.

Intentionally or not, the producers of *King Kong* encourage this identification by etching the character of Kong with keen sympathy. For the ape is a figure in a tradition familiar to moviegoers; the tradition of the pitiable monster. We think of Lon Chaney in the role of Quasimodo, of Karloff in the original *Frankenstein*. As we watch the Frankenstein monster's fumbling and disastrous attempts to befriend a flower-picking child, our sympathies are enlisted with the monster in his impenetrable loneliness. And so with Kong. As he roars in his chains, while barkers sell tickets to boobs who gape at him, we perhaps feel something more deep than pathos. We begin to sense something of the problem that engaged Eugene O'Neill in *The Hairy Ape*: the dilemma of an animal spirit forced to live in a jungle built by machines.

King Kong, it is true, had special relevance in 1933. Landscapes of the depression are glimpsed early in the film when an impresario, seeking some desperate pretty girl to play the lead in a jungle movie, visits souplines and a Woman's Home Mission. In Fay Wray—who's been caught snitching an apple from a fruitstand—his search is ended. When he gives her a big feed and a movie contract, the girl is magic-carpeted out of the world of the National Recovery Act. And when, in the film's climax, Kong smashes that very Third Avenue landscape in which Fay had wandered hungry, audiences of 1933 may well have felt a personal satisfaction.

What is curious is that audiences of 1960 remain hooked. For in the heart of urban man, one suspects, lurks the impulse to fling a bomb. Though machines speed him to the scene of his daily grind, though IBM comptometers ("freeing the human mind from drudgery") enable him to drudge more efficiently once he arrives, there comes a moment when he wishes to turn upon his machines and kick hell out of them. He wants to hurl his combination radio-alarm clock out the bedroom window and listen to its smash. What subway commuter wouldn't love—just for once—to see the downtown express smack head-on into the uptown local? Such a wish is gratified in that memorable scene in *Kong* that opens with a wide-angle shot: interior of a railway car on the Third Avenue El. Straphangers are nodding, the literate refold their newspapers. Unknown to them, Kong has torn away a section of trestle toward which the train now speeds. The motorman spies Kong up ahead, jams on the brakes. Passengers hurtle together like so many peas in a pail. In a window of the car appear Kong's bloodshot eyes. Women shriek. Kong picks up the railway car as if it were a rat, flips it to the street and ties knots in it, or something. To any commuter the scene must appear one of the most satisfactory pieces of celluloid ever exposed.

Yet however violent his acts, Kong remains a gentleman. Remarkable is his sense of chivalry. Whenever a fresh boa constrictor threatens Fay, Kong first sees that the lady is safely parked, then manfully thrashes her attacker. (And she, the ingrate, runs away every time his back is turned.) Atop the Empire State Building, ignoring his pursuers, Kong places Fay on a ledge as tenderly as if she were a dozen eggs. He fondles her, then turns to face the Army Air Force. And Kong is perhaps the most disinterested lover since Cyrano; his attentions to the lady are utterly without hope of reward. After all, between a five-foot blonde and a fifty-foot ape, love can hardly be more than an intellectual flirtation. In his simian way King Kong is the hopelessly yearning lover of Petrarchan convention. His forced exit from his jungle, in chains, results directly from his single-minded pursuit of Fay. He smashes a Broadway theater when the notion enters his dull brain that the flashbulbs of photographers somehow endanger the lady. His perilous shinnying up a skyscraper to pluck Fay from her boudoir is an act of the kindliest of hearts. He's impossible to discourage even though the love of his life can't lay eyes on him without shrieking murder.

The tragedy of King Kong then, is to be the beast who at the end of the fable fails to turn into the handsome prince. This is the conviction that the scriptwriters would leave with us in the film's closing line. As Kong's corpse lies blocking traffic in the street, the enterpreneur who brought Kong to New York turns to the assembled reporters and proclaims: "That's your story, boys—it was Beauty killed the Beast!" But greater forces than those of the screaming Lady have combined to lay Kong low, if you ask me Kong lives for a time as one of those persecuted near-animal souls bewildered in the middle of an industrial order, whose simple desires are thwarted at every turn. He climbs the Empire State Building because in all New York it's the closest thing he can find to the clifftop of his jungle isle. He dies, a pitiful dolt, and the army brass and publicity-men cackle over him. His death is the only possible outcome to as neat a tragic dilemma as you can ask for. The machine-guns do him in, while the manicured human hero (a nice clean Dartmouth boy) carries away Kong's sweetheart to the altar. O, the misery of it all. There's far more truth about upper-middle class American life in *King Kong* than in the last seven dozen novels of John P. Marquand.

A negro friend from Atlanta tells me that in movie houses in colored neighborhoods throughout the South, *Kong* does a constant business. They show the thing in Atlanta at least every year, presumably to the same audiences. Perhaps this popularity may simply be due to the fact that Kong is one of the most watchable movies ever constructed, but I wonder whether Negro audiences may not find some archetypal appeal in this serio-comic tale of a huge black powerful free spirit whom all the hard-working white policemen are out to kill.

Every day in the week on a screen somewhere in the world, King Kong relives his agony. Again and again he expires on the Empire State Building, as audiences of the devout assist his sacrifice. We watch him die, and by extension kill the ape within our bones, but these little deaths of ours occur in prosaic surroundings. We do not die on a tower, New York before our feet, nor do we give our lives to smash a few flying machines. It is not for us to bring to a momentary standstill the civilization in which we move. King Kong does this for us. And so we kill him again and again, in much-spliced celluloid, while the ape in us expires from day to day, obscure, in desperation.

Questions

1. The movie *King Kong*:

    a. has been seen by more Americans than have seen a performance of *Hamlet*
    b. has made the legend of the monster ape King Kong unkillable
    c. lured a large segment of the television viewing audience away from powerful competition in 1955.
    d. all of the above

2. *King Kong* is:

    a. filled with plodding mummies
    b. known to have been produced in Ethiopia
    c. insignificant compared with the other great movies of the times
    d. filled with good healthy sadism

3. *King Kong* was produced by:

    a. Cooper and Schoedsack
    b. Warner Brothers
    c. Universal Studios
    b. both a and c

4. King Kong's huge advantage over giant ants and walking vegetables is:

   a. his being a pterodactyl
   b. his simian nature
   c. clearly evident in Eugene O'Neill's writings
   d. his wide armspan

5. *King Kong* fits into the tradition of:

   a. Dr. Jekyll and Mr. Hyde
   b. the giant from the great unknown
   c. the pitiable monster
   d. the beast and the beauty

6. Kong smashed the Third Avenue landscape in which:

   a. was found the Women's Home Mission
   b. the leading lady had been discovered
   c. soup and breadlines of the depression were first started
   d. today is found the theater which premiered *King Kong*

7. In the man of 1960, there lurked the impulse to:

   a. befriend a flower-picking child
   b. snitch an apple from a fruitstand
   c. love
   d. fling a bomb

8. Kong's sense of chivalry is evident when he:

   a. put Fay on the ledge of the Empire State Building
   b. picked up the railway car
   c. becomes a disinterested lover
   d. picked the nurse out of a burning building

9. King Kong climbed the Empire State Building because:

   a. he wanted to escape from attack
   b. he wanted to save Fay
   c. it reminded him of something from his home
   d. it was closer to his size than anything else

10. *King Kong* may have some archetypal appeal to:

 a. Negro audiences in the South
 b. middle-class children
 c. Negro audiences in the North
 d. all lower-class Americans

Answers

1.	a	6.	b
2.	d	7.	d
3.	a	8.	a
4.	b	9.	c
5.	c	10.	a

Which Pattern Do You Like?

Now that you have tried all nine pacing patterns, is one pattern better for you than another? Why do you feel that this pattern helps you read faster? After practicing all of the new motions, especially work on the one or two pacing motions with which you feel most comfortable. For further improvement of your reading skills, consider the following suggestions:

1. Use each new technique you learn on the explanations and discussions of rapid reading in this guide. New skills can be effective if you use them.
2. Besides using your reading skills on light reading such as novels, apply rapid reading techniques to all your outside reading. This includes correspondence, newspapers, magazines, and anything else that you normally read during a day.
3. More important than anything else, is to set aside a specific time period every day for practicing your rapid reading. Thirty minutes of daily rapid reading practice is enough to ensure steady progress. Although any reading material will do, it is best to begin with easy material and gradually work up to a more difficult level.

Remember, always use a pacing pattern when you read. By the way, did you pace while reading this page?

Reading Groups of Words

In the following section you will overcome word-by-word reading and instead learn how to see large groups of words. This skill is learned in several stages, all of which should be carefully considered.

1. Space reading
2. Circling
3. Slashing
4. Grouper card
5. Eye stretch
6. Eye swing

Span of Perception — Fixations

Many people hinder themselves from using their full reading potential because they use their eyes inefficiently. Their span of perception is very short because they only see one or two syllables per fixation, instead of learning to perceive phrases from two to four words at a single glance. The following illustrates a poor reader's perception pattern:

Mr. Barbing sat in his rocking chair thinking about his

childhood. It didn't seem possible that the years had

passed so quickly. He could still remember his high

school days when he had squirted the ink from his inkwell

across the classroom with his quill. College was only a

flashing memory. Even the many years he had put in with

the firm no longer seemed significant. Life had passed

too quickly.

A fixation, or a point at which the eyes stop, is represented by each dot, while the arc indicates the span of perception for that point. To see the span of perception for an efficient reader, note the following paragraph, where the eyes swing farther in each glance:

Mr. Barbing sat in his rocking chair thinking about his

childhood. It didn't seem possible that the years had

passed so quickly. He could still remember his high

school days when he had squirted the ink from his inkwell

across the classroom with his quill. College was only a

flashing memory. Even the many years he had put in with

the firm no longer seemed significant. Life had passed

too quickly.

Now look back over the perception pattern on this page. Try to see each phrase with one glance. Focus your eyes on the dot instead of directly looking at the words.

Span of Perception — Fixation Paragraph

The next paragraph in this book will help you measure your present span of perception. First ask someone to assist you. Then using a pencil, poke a hole in the page where it is indicated (☆). Now ask your partner to look through the hole and watch your eye movement while you read the next paragraph aloud.

Have some one hold this up for you to read aloud. Your partner will look through the hole at your eyes. He will see your eyes move across the line in a series of quick jerks (fixations). His job is to count the average number of fixations per line. The average person has

from five to seven fixations per line. If you have fewer than that your eye span is better than average. Since these are four-inch lines, a person with an average of four fixations per line can take in about an inch of print. As you continue rapid reading, periodically use the fixation sheet or one of your own making.

Now, have your partner read the above paragraph while you watch his eyes to see how the eyes work.

Read Above the Line

Now you will practice the first exercise in building an increased span of perception: *space reading.* In order for you to stop focusing on individual words and to encourage you to broaden your perception to take in groups of words, it is important that you learn to *read above the line.* Try to develop this new skill by looking only at the dot above each phrase on the page below. You will be able to see the phrase without looking directly at it. Practice space reading the following phrases at least ten times.

•
The log cabin

•
lay hidden

•
so that

•
surrounded by shrubs

•
from human view

•
its inhabitants

lived quietly

away from

the humdrum

of rushing society

If ever

you met

the couple

that lived

within this quaint

little log cabin

you would

undoubtedly feel

your problems

were not really

as frightening

as you thought

Now take any page in your novel, dot all the phrases (any group of words that look like they go together) and practice space reading. Try putting the dots in every two words at first, and then after a few lines put in dots for every three words, and continue this "stretching" until you are attempting to see each line in a maximum of three phrases. After you feel you can comfortably do this, try space reading without dots, looking into the space directly above the phrase you are trying to see.

One word of caution: Don't expect to practice phrase reading for a few minutes and thus have mastered the technique. Daily practice is required if you are to stretch your normal span of perceptions. Ten minutes a day spent practicing grouping drills is a good investment.

Circling

So that reading phrases instead of individual words becomes natural to you, we are providing you with a circling exercise. While pacing in the following paragraph look at the circles instead of the words. Practice reading phrase after phrase as fast as you can until your eyes relax and feel comfortable in seeing words in groups.

I have known both of you all your lives, have carried your Daddy in my arms and on my shoulders kissed and spanked him and watched him learn to walk. I don't know if you've know anybody from that far back, if you've loved anybody that long first as an infant, then as a child, then as a man, you gain a strange perspective on time and human pain and effort.

Now go back over the material you have already read in this guide and choose a passage and divide the words into meaningful phrases by circling them. The phrases don't have to be grammatically correct units, but should be one-half inch to two inches long.

Circle phrases for approximately ten minutes. Then practice focusing your eyes on the circles, hopping your eyes from one circle to the next. Repeat this exercise until your eyes become a little more adept at taking in phrases. The repetition will gradually accustom you to *think* groups of words, as well as to *physically see* groups. Begin circling.

NOTE: Don't begin any other drills until you are certain that you are beginning to read groups of words. If you feel you are not able to read in phrases at all, go back to the beginning of span-of-perception instruction and start over.

Slashing

If you are beginning to feel that you are no longer struggling to overcome fixation on individual words, you are ready for the following exercise. Practice on the following drill perceiving each phrase with only one glance. Each new phrase is separated by a slash. Remember, use a pacing motion to point at each phrase and look above the phrase, not directly at it.

The thunderous roar/of crashing waves/upon/the jutting edge/of the rocky precipice/echoed in my mind/as I stood alone on the opposing/shore/remembering/the love/I had lost. Reflecting upon/the movement of joy/I had shared/in the past, my cold/and shivering body/became intoxicated/with the warmth of memory./Even if/there was a storm,/I could see the calm rising/of a restful dawn.

Repeat this exercise at least ten times before continuing. The repetition causes monotony; the monotony will cause you to relax and thus perceive phrases a little easier. Once you are in the *habit* of looking for groups, rather than looking for individual words, half the grouping battle is won.

The Grouper Card

An advanced grouper card is provided for you. Its purpose is twofold: to increase speed and span of perception and to develop efficient eye-swing movements. After you cut it out, follow the instructions printed on it and practice reading with it on your novel or other printed materials. Using the grouper card will help you see more words at a glance and decrease the time it takes you to see words, thus dramatically increasing your reading speed. If all you do is learn to see two words at a time instead of the one word you normally see at each fixation, your speed will double and you will have better comprehension. The two-hole part of the grouper will help you to develop efficient eye swing. If you practice daily for only a few minutes, you'll see definite progress in only a few weeks.

Using any reading material, cut out the grouper card from the back of this book and begin to read.

GROUPER CARD

						(remove)						

1. Cut out center rectangle.
2. Guide grouper down center of page.
3. As eyes become accustomed to seeing all the words, extend the opening.

(remove)							(remove)

1. Cut out end rectangles.
2. As you guide grouper down page, swing eyes from phrase to phrase.
3. Increase the size of the openings as you are able.

"Eye Stretching"

With proper training, your eye may be able to see and comprehend common print phrases up to two inches in length. The following exercises will provide you with such training so that your perception of phrases will be "stretched," enabling you to increase your present grouping abilities.

Exercise 1

In the following exercise, the object is to read each line of numbers by focusing only on the dot in the middle of the line. Using a separate sheet of paper, write down the numbers you perceive in each line as you focus *only* on the dot. Do not look at the numbers directly. You will discover that each time you repeat the exercise, you will see more numbers on each side of the dot. Practice until your peripheral vision comprehends as much of the line as physically possible for you (after you have repeated this exercise five times you will probably be at your physical limits).

9 8 5 2 8 5 4 0 1 · 0 7 5 4 8 6 2 8 2

1 4 7 0 9 7 4 2 0 · 7 4 1 2 9 0 8 4 3

0 8 9 6 7 4 2 3 0 · 1 7 0 5 3 7 9 8 3

8 6 4 8 0 3 2 1 8 · 0 1 4 2 6 8 4 2 9

9 7 5 0 8 8 3 5 7 · 7 4 9 8 2 2 4 8 0

7 8 4 7 5 3 9 0 2 · 0 7 3 5 1 4 9 0 6

2 3 5 4 6 9 9 6 1 · 9 9 7 4 5 3 4 9 0

0 9 7 6 4 3 7 6 5 · 9 5 3 3 1 4 7 8 6

8 7 4 9 8 4 2 3 4 · 9 6 4 2 7 5 3 8 0

5 8 7 3 1 4 6 8 0 · 4 9 6 4 3 2 6 8 0

5 7 8 9 4 7 6 3 1 · 7 8 9 0 8 5 3 2 6

0 8 6 4 2 1 3 4 6 · 3 2 7 8 9 8 6 4 2

8 6 4 3 2 5 4 8 9 · 7 5 4 7 6 8 9 0 3

2 4 5 7 9 0 7 8 6 · 3 2 3 5 7 8 9 9 1

0 9 7 5 3 5 7 8 9 · 3 2 4 2 1 4 5 6 3

Exercise 2

Now focus your eyes on letters instead of numbers and repeat the exercise, again looking only on the dots. You will quickly observe that letters are easier to see for most people than numbers.

Q W S C F T Y H N · K O L B K U Y G V

X F G B H U J N M · O L M Y T F C D E

P I U Y R E W Q A · D F G H J K L M N

```
L K J H G F D S A · X C V B N M P O I

Z X C V B N M A S · F G H J K L O I U

H G F D V C X Z Q · E R O I U Y H J K

L P O K M N J I U · B V G Y T F C X D

R E S Z A W Q A Z · W E D C F T Y H N

Z A Q S X C D W E · V B G R T H N M J

M J Y U I K L O P · I Y T R E W Q A S

W E R T Y U I O K · H G F D S X C V B
```

Exercise 3

For something a little more challenging, try the following exercise which contains symbols that may be difficult

```
! # " $ % — & ' (    ' & — ) : ? , * @

* ) ' & % $ # " !,   @ : + ) ' & % $ #

/ ¢ ' & % & ( ) *    $ " ! # % & ( * '

! & ) ' — $ ' # %    ( * + @ ? ! & — (

@ + * ) ' & % $ #    # $ % & ( * + ! :

; ¢ / = / ¢ ( & %    — ' :/ ! ; ¢ = — :

* + & % $ # — ' (    ? @ % " ! # % $ &

. ? @ # ) ' — % $    " — ' ) * + @ . ?

— $ # " $ % — & (    + : . , ! # " % '

& & % $ ( * @ $ /    ¢ = — . , / 0 & $
```

to duplicate. Try to duplicate the symbols on a separate sheet of paper, looking only at the center line.

Eye Swing

Once you begin learning to see groups of words at one fixation, the next goal is to develop a rhythmic eye-swing from group to group across the page. The following exercises will assist you in developing this desired skill.

Exercise 4

Swing your eyes from cluster to cluster in Fig. 5-1 at a steady pace. Since you are looking at numbers and letters

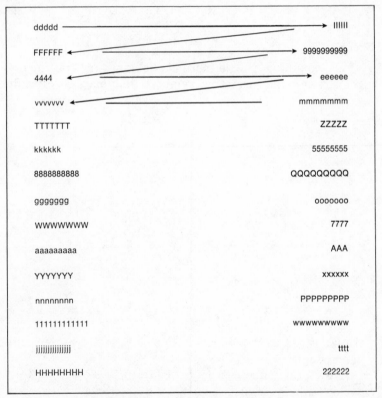

Fig. 5-1. First eye-swing exercise.

instead of blocks, go slowly enough to comprehend what is there. After glancing at a couple of lines, take a sheet of paper and write down the exact letters and numbers you have just read. Repeat this exercise ten times.

Exercise 5

Now apply your new reading technique on phrases using the pacing movement as you read. The object of the exer-

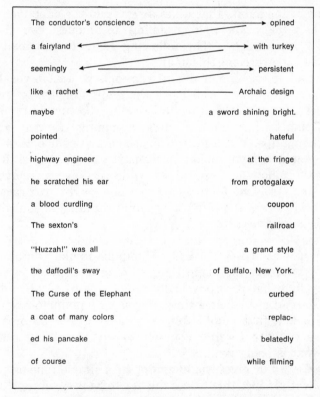

The conductor's conscience ──────────────→ opined

a fairyland ←────────────────→ with turkey

seemingly ←──────────────→ persistent

like a rachet ←────────────── Archaic design

maybe   a sword shining bright.

pointed   hateful

highway engineer   at the fringe

he scratched his ear   from protogalaxy

a blood curdling   coupon

The sexton's   railroad

"Huzzah!" was all   a grand style

the daffodil's sway   of Buffalo, New York.

The Curse of the Elephant   curbed

a coat of many colors   replac-

ed his pancake   belatedly

of course   while filming

Fig. 5-2. Second eye-swing exercise.

cise in Fig. 5-2 is to achieve a smooth return sweep while perceiving each phrase before moving on to the next.

Now practicing rhythmic reading in your novel. Spend five or ten minutes concentrating on hopping your eyes with a smooth motion. Use a pacing motion.

6

Vocalizing and Its Cures

One of the habits that takes away from the effectiveness of the acceleration and grouping techniques you have learned, is vocalizing. The following remarks will explain how you can overcome this habit.

Should you be one of the many people who have vocalizing difficulties, those who move their lips, tongue, or even whisper the words that they are reading, be sure to try the cures suggested: mumble-reading, humming, chewing gum or touching lips. These cures are also effective for determining if you have a vocalizing problem. If you are unable to do easily the following four things while reading, you have a vocalizing problem to some degree and ought to practice these cures every day for a few minutes until you find that you no longer vocalize.

Mumble-reading involves repeating aloud a meaningless phrase such as "1-2-3," "1-2-3" or "mumbo-jumbo," "mumbo-jumbo" while at the same time reading silently. You will quickly find that it is physically impossible to vocalize and mumble-read at the same time. If you keep mumble-reading you will find that your habit of vocalizing will be broken because you are forcing yourself to say something other than what is being read.

Humming involves the humming of a simple tune as you read silently. Since this forces the lips to be pressed together most of the time it is especially effective for people who find they are lip movers. This humming technique keeps the lip-moving reader from silently forming the words with his mouth as he reads.

Chewing gum is an easy exercise and very effective. Chew several (three or more) sticks of gum at the same time with a rhythmic, cud-chewing motion. This will involve all parts of your mouth in guiding the gum, swallowing the juices, and will make it very difficult for you to chew and still vocalize while you are reading.

Touching lips simply requires you to place your fingers lightly on your lips as you read silently. Any lip-moving will be obvious and you can then make yourself doubly conscious of it by pressing slightly on your lips each time you catch yourself vocalizing.

REMEMBER: Vocalizing is a bad habit and like all habits is correctable as long as you make yourself aware of it when you catch yourself vocalizing. Now turn to any section you have already read, and practice one of the suggested cures for several minutes.

7

Techniques
for Increased Efficiency

Comprehension Building

There are essentially two main ways to build comprehension:

1. *Question before reading.* The reader must always be conscious of comprehension as he reads and this can best be accomplished by reading with a questioning mind. We have all been in situations, perhaps even in school classes, where we have been asked to read specific pages in preparation for the next class. And we did the reading. But at the next class when we were questioned on the contents of those pages, it seemed that we didn't know much. Has this happened to you? Sure. But, how different it was those few times that the teacher asked us to read specific pages, but also indicated what it was that we should look for: "Discover the route that the Crusaders took on the First Crusade." "Who were the people that they came in contact with?" "Where were the first five battles fought?" And so on. What difference did it make when you were questioned the next class? A tremendous difference! You knew three times as much as you normally knew. What was the difference? *You were reading with a questioning mind.* You were reading with a purpose, and not just passing your eyes over pages passively. Awareness of your purpose tells you when you can skim and when you can safely skip things altogether. The reader must raise questions about his reading material *before* he begins read-

ing. What does he want to get from his reading? What does he want to know? What is the thesis or problem here? What is the purpose of this work? What is the main sequence of ideas? What particular things will he be hunting for in this work? By raising questions like these before he reads, when he comes across the answers they will stand out, and they will be remembered.

2. *Preview and postview*. If a reader will preview quickly the material he is about to read, that is, take a couple of minutes to glance briefly at each page (using an Arrow or Zig-Zag pattern) before reading, he will get an overview of the contents in terms of main ideas, thesis, style, significant illustrations, etc., which will give greater understanding of the materials when read. The effect of this is to give the reader a feeling of confidence and assurance, thus increasing speed and comprehension. The reader feels as if he is covering familiar territory. This *prereading* also enables him to discard useless material without wasting time reading it for detail. Prereading is also an essential step in defining your precise purpose in reading a particular work. Prereading will also indicate when the content is familiar, is irrelevant to your purpose, or too technical for you to handle, and thus can be safely skipped.

This previewing and then reading should always be followed by *postviewing* of the material. Postviewing is simply previewing *after* you have finished reading, and its purpose is to note for a second time the important points that were covered during the reading. The rapid review of the contents in just a minute or two will reinforce the key points and main issues of the reading and will aid retention.

You can become the world's fastest reader, but if you don't know what you have read, your rapid reading skill will be of no use to you. So that you will be able to read faster and maintain good comprehension, we will encourage you to develop the habit of skimming (one way of previewing) and scanning after you read, which will give you an overview of the material and a broader understanding of key points. The techniques of skimming and scanning are covered next.

Skimming

Skimming is defined as reading unfamiliar material, looking for main ideas.

You will be able to rapidly perceive *the main ideas of a book,* chapter, report, or article by merely skimming instead of reading the material from beginning to end. How does a person skim? Develop the habit of *rapidly reading the first sentence* of each paragraph which is nearly always the topic sentence (the sentence which spells out the most important point in the paragraph). This will enable you to have a basic understanding of the important ideas in the work, at a speed five or six times as fast as you normally could read the material. As you rush through the work skimming, don't allow yourself to read the details of any paragraphs, only topic sentences. You are reading for ideas now, not details.

Time yourself as you skim your next reading selection in this book. Immediately after you finish reading, write down the main idea of the article in a few sentences.

A Trifling Incident
by Henry Fielding

Tom Jones, when very young, had presented Sophia with a little bird, which he had taken from the nest, had nursed up, and taught to sing.

Of this bird, Sophia, then about thirteen years old, was so extremely fond, that her chief business was to feed and tend it, and her chief pleasure to play with it. By these means little Tommy, for so the bird was called, was become so tame, that it would feed out of the hand of its mistress, would perch upon the finger, and lie contented in her bosom, where it seemed almost sensible of its own happiness; though she always kept a small string about its leg, nor would ever trust it with the liberty of flying away.

One day, when Mr. Allworthy and his whole family dined at Mr. Western's, Master Blifil, being in the garden with little Sophia, and observing the extreme fondness that she showed for her little bird, desired her to trust it for a moment in his hands. Sophia presently complied with the young gentleman's request, and after some previous caution, delivered him her bird; of which he was no sooner in possession, than he slipped the string from its leg and tossed it into the air.

The foolish animal no sooner perceived itself at liberty, than forgetting all the favors it had received from Sophia, it flew directly from her, and perched on a bough at some distance.

Sophia, seeing her bird gone, screamed out so loud, that Tom Jones, who was at a little distance, immediately ran to her assistance.

He was no sooner informed of what had happened, than he cursed Blifil for a pitiful malicious rascal; and then immediately stripping off his coat he applied himself to climbing the tree to which the bird escaped.

Tom had almost recovered his little namesake, when the branch on which it was perched, and that hung over a canal, broke, and the poor lad plumped over head and ears into the water.

Sophia's concern now changed its object. And as she apprehended the boy's life was in danger, she screamed ten times louder than before; and indeed Master Blifil himself now seconded her with all the vociferation in his power.

The company, who were sitting in a room next the garden, were instantly alarmed, and came all forth; but just as they reached the canal, Tom (for the water was luckily pretty shallow in that part) arrived safely on shore.

Thwackum fell violently on poor Tom, who stood drooping and shivering before him, when Mr. Allworthy desired him to have patience; and turning to Master Blifil, said, "Pray, child, what is the reason of all this disturbance?"

Master Blifil answered, "Indeed, uncle, I am very sorry for what I have done; I have been unhappily the occasion of it all. I had Miss Sophia's bird in my hand,

and thinking the poor creature languished for liberty, I own I could not forbear giving it what it desired; for I always thought there was something very cruel in confining anything. It seemed to be against the law of nature, by which everything has a right to liberty; nay, it is even unchristian, for it is not doing what we would be done by; but if I had imagined Miss Sophia would have been so much concerned at it, I am sure I never would have done it; nay, if I had known what would have happened to the bird itself; for when Master Jones, who climbed up that tree after it, fell into the water, the bird took a second flight, and presently a nasty hawk carried it away."

Poor Sophia, who had now first heard of her little Tommy's fate (for her concern for Jones had prevented her perceiving it when it happened), shed a shower of tears. These Mr. Allworthy endeavored to assuage, promising her a much finer bird; but she declared she would never have another. Her father chid her for crying so for a foolish bird; but could not help telling young Blifil, if he was a son of his, his backside should be well flead.

Sophia now returned to her chamber, the two young gentlemen were sent home, and the rest of the company returned to their bottle; where a conversation ensued on the subject of the bird, so curious, that we think it deserves a chapter by itself.

Square had no sooner lighted his pipe, than, addressing himself to Allworthy, he thus began: "Sir, I cannot help congratulating you on your nephew; who, at an age when few lads have any ideas but of sensible objects, is arrived at a capacity of distinguishing right from wrong. To confine anything, seems to me against the law of nature, by which everything hath a right to liberty. These were his words; and the impression they have made on me is never to be eradicated. Can any man have a higher notion of the rule of right and the eternal fitness of things? I cannot help promising myself, from such a dawn, that the meridian of this youth will be equal to that of either the elder or the younger Brutus."

Here Thwackum hastily interrupted, and spilling some of his wine, and swallowing the rest with great eagerness, answered, "From another expression he made use of, I hope he will resemble much better men. The law of nature is a jargon of words, which means nothing. I know not of any such law, nor of any right which can be derived from it. To do as we would be done by, is indeed a Christian motive, as the boy well expressed himself; and I am glad to find my instructions have borne such good fruit."

"If vanity was a thing fit," says Square, "I might indulge some on the same occasion; for whence only he can have learnt his notions of right or wrong, I think is pretty apparent. If there be no law of nature, there is no right nor wrong."

"How!" says the parson, "do you then banish revelation? Am I talking with a deist or an atheist?"

"Drink about," says Western. "Pox of your laws of nature! I don't know what you mean, either of you, by right and wrong. To take away my girl's bird was wrong, in my opinion; and my neighbor Allworthy may do as he pleases; but to encourage boys in such practices is to breed them up to the gallows."

Allworthy answered, "That he was sorry for what his nephew had done, but could not consent to punish him, as he acted rather from a generous than unworthy motive." He said, "If the boy had stolen the bird, none would have been more ready to vote for a severe chastisement than himself; but it was plain that was not his design;" and indeed, it was as apparent to him, that he could have no other views but what he had himself avowed. (For as to that malicious purpose which Sophia suspected, it never once entered into the head of Mr. Allworthy.) He at length concluded with again blaming the action as inconsiderate, and which, he said, was pardonable only in a child.

Square had delivered his opinion so openly, that if he was now silent, he must submit to have his judgment censured. He said, therefore, with some warmth, "That

Mr. Allworthy had too much respect to the dirty consid-
eration of property. That in passing our judgments on
great and mighty actions, all private regards should be
laid aside; for by adhering to those narrow rules, the
younger Brutus had been condemned of ingratitude, and
the elder of parricide."

"And if they had been hanged too for those crimes,"
cried Thwackum, "they would have no more than their
deserts. A couple of heathenish villains! Heaven be
praised we have no Brutuses nowadays! I wish, Mr.
Square, you would desist from filling the minds of my
pupils with such antichristian stuff; for the consequence
must be, while they are under my care, its being well
scourged out of them again. There is your disciple Tom
almost spoiled already. I overheard him the other day
disputing with Master Blifil that there was no merit in
faith without works. I know that is one of your tenets,
and I suppose he had it from you."

"Don't accuse me of spoiling him," says Square.
"Who taught him to laugh at whatever is virtuous and
decent, and fit and right in the nature of things? He is
your own scholar, and I disclaim him. No. no, Master
Blifil is my boy. Young as he is, that lad's notions of
moral rectitude I defy you ever to eradicate."

Thwackum put on a contemptuous sneer at this, and
replied, "Ay, ay, I will venture him with you. He is too
well grounded for all your philosophical cant to hurt. No,
no, I have taken care to instil such principles into him—"

"And I have instilled principles into him too," cries
Square. "What but the sublime idea of virtue could inspire a human mind with the generous thought of giving
liberty? And I repeat to you again, if it was a fit thing
to be proud, I might claim the honor of having infused
that idea."

"And if pride was not forbidden," said Thwackum,
"I might boast of having taught him that duty which he
himself assigned as his motive."

"So between you both," says the squire, "The young
gentleman hath been taught to rob my daughter of her

bird. I find I must take care of my partridge-mew. I shall have some virtuous religious man or other set all my partridges at liberty." Then slapping a gentleman of the law, who was present on the back, he cried out, "What say you to this, Mr. Counsellor? Is not this against law?"

The lawyer with great gravity delivered himself as follows:

"If the case be put of a partridge, there can be no doubt but an action would lie; for though this be *ferae naturae*, yet being reclaimed, property vests: but being the case of a singing bird, though reclaimed, as it is a thing of base nature, it must be considered as *nullius in bonis*. In this case, therefore, I conceive the plaintiff must be non-suited; and I should disadvise the bringing any such action."

"Well," says the squire, "if it be *nullus bonus,* let us drink about, and talk a little of the state of the nation, or some such discourse that we all understand; for I am sure I don't understand a word of this. It may be learning and sense for aught I know; but you shall never persuade me into it. Pox! you have neither of you mentioned a word of that poor lad who deserves to be commended: to venture breaking his neck to oblige my girl was a generous-spirited action: I have learning enough to see that. D—n me, here's Tom's health! I shall love the boy for it the longest day I have to live."

Thus was the debate interrupted; but it would probably have been soon resumed, had not Mr. Allworthy presently called for his coach and carried off the two combatants.

Such was the conclusion of this adventure of the bird, and of the dialogue occasioned by it; which we could not help recounting to our reader, though it happened some years before that stage or period of time at which our history is now arrived.

Questions

1. The gift was presented to Sophia by:

   a. Henry Fielding
   b. Tom Jones
   c. Mr. Allworthy
   d. Master Blifil

2. At the time of the incident recorded here Sophia was about _____ years old.

   a. 12
   b. 14
   c. 17
   d. 13

3. Sophia's feeling about the bird was:

   a. extreme fondness
   b. occasional interest
   c. indifference
   d. disgust

4. The bird escaped when:

   a. Sophia left the cage open
   b. Tom dropped it from its nest
   c. Master Blifil released the string attached to its leg
   d. Mr. Webster left the window open and it flew out into the meadow

5. Tom had nearly recovered the bird when:

   a. he fell into a canal
   b. the branch broke
   c. a hawk carried it away
   d. all of the above

6. In the conversation that ensued, the first opinion of the incident upheld the boy's ability to:

   a. distinguish right from wrong
   b. follow the laws of nature
   c. pursue the right of liberty
   d. all of the above

7. The uncle would not punish the boy for releasing the bird because:

    a. he was not sorry for what the boy had done
    b. he felt the motive was just
    c. it was an accident
    d. no one was injured

8. Master Blifil is compared to what historic figure?

    a. Ceasar
    b. Brutus
    c. Nero
    d. Hamlet

9. The debate ended when:

    a. the counsellor left to release his partridges
    b. the lawyer broke the table with his fist
    c. it developed into a brawl
    d. the squire pledged to love Tom for his deed

10. Which of the following was involved in the story?

    a. Circle
    b. West
    c. Thwackum
    d. all of the above

Answers

1.	b	6.	d
2.	d	7.	b
3.	a	8.	b
4.	c	9.	d
5.	d	10.	c

From now on always preview and postview everything you read, both in this course and in your outside reading. Spend at least twenty seconds previewing and the same amount of time postviewing each reading selection as you practice. Also, make certain that you always preview and postview reading matter that is part of your everyday reading.

Since you will want to adapt skimming and scanning to your reading needs, feel free to experiment with these techniques.

Enter your speed and comprehension for the last selection on your record sheet and compare this score with all the others you have listed. Has your rapid reading progressively improved? Don't be discouraged if your score seems to be jumping up and down. That often happens when you are first learning to read faster. The general trend on your record sheet should be moving gradually up the chart.

A Method for Marking Material

Most of us like to read with a pen in our hand so that we can mark important ideas or facts as we come to them. This combination of reading and marking is an aid to our comprehension because it serves to focus our attention on what we are reading. The problem with reading like this is that few of us have learned a system for marking materials and thus have fallen into a habit of simply underlining everything. Reviewing material that we have marked this way is quite complicated because we must reread everything in order to find out the relative importance of the marked material. To avoid this, learn the following marking system and use it whenever you read. The result will be an improved and speeded-up organization and review of material read.

_____ For major concepts such as a thesis sentence, underline with a solid line. Anything that is of primary importance may be indicated this way.

------- Indicate material that is of secondary importance with a broken line. This includes material that is important but not of sufficient importance to be considered key.

①② To indicate things in a series or items which follow in a given order, use circled numbers.

[ ] Brackets are useful in indicating material that may be excerpted or quoted at a later time.

* Use an asterisk in the margin to indicate an interesting sentence or statement.

? Use a question mark to indicate anything that you find questionable or puzzling.

◯ Circle individual words or phrases which are new or strange—in general, anything that needs to be looked up in a dictionary.

(( )) To indicate summary sentences, enclose the entire sentence in double parentheses.

A
D To indicate agreement or disagreement with what is being said, use either the letter A (agree) or D (disagree) in the margin.

Try this new marking system on the following reading.

The American Crisis
by Thomas Paine

These are the times that try men's souls: The summer soldier and the sunshine patriot will in this crisis, shrink from the service of his country; but he that stands it Now, deserves the love and thanks of man and woman. Tyranny, like hell, is not easily conquered; yet we have this consolation with us, that the harder the conflict, the more glorious the triumph. What we obtain too cheap, we esteem to[o] lightly:——'Tis dearness only that gives everything its value. Heaven knows how to put a proper price upon its goods; and it would be strange indeed, if so celestial and article as FREEDOM should not be highly rated. Britain, with an army to enforce her tyranny, has declared that she has a right (not only to) TAX but "to BIND *us in* ALL CASES WHATSOEVER," and if being *bound in that manner,* is not slavery then is there not such a thing as slavery upon earth. Even the expression is impious for so unlimited a power can belong only to God.

Whether the Independence of the Continent was declared too soon, or delayed too long, I will not now enter into as an argument; my own simple opinion is, that had it been eight months earlier, it would have been much better. We did not make a proper use of last winter, neither could we, while we were in a dependent state. However, the fault, if it were one, was all our own; we have none to blame but ourselves. But no great deal is lost yet; all that Howe has been doing for this month past, is rather a ravage than a conquest, which the spirit of the Jersies a year ago would have quickly repulsed, and which time and a little resolution will soon recover.

I have as little superstition in me as any man living, but my secret opinion has ever been, and still is, that God Almighty will not give up a people to military destruction, or leave them unsupportedly to perish, who have so earnestly and so repeatedly sought to avoid the calamities of war, by every decent method which wisdom could invent. Neither have I so much of the infidel in me, as to suppose that he has relinquished the government of the world, and given us up to the care of devils; and as I do not, I cannot see on what grounds the king of Britain can look up to heaven for help against us: a common murderer, a highwayman, or a house-breaker, has as good a pretence as he.

'Tis surprising to see how rapidly a panic will sometimes run through a country. All nations and ages have been subject to them: Britain has trembled like an ague at the report of a French fleet of flat-bottomed boats; and in the fourteenth century the whole English army, after ravaging the kingdom of France, was driven back like men petrified with fear; and this brave exploit was performed by a few broken forces collected and headed by a woman, Joan of Arc. Would that heaven might inspire some Jersey maid to spirit up her countrymen, and save her fair fellow sufferers from ravage and ravishment! Yet panics, in some cases, have their uses; they produce as much good as hurt. Their duration is always short; the mind soon grows through them, and acquires a firmer habit than before. But their peculiar advantage is, that they are the touchstones of sincerity and hypocrisy, and bring things and men to light, which might otherwise have lain forever undiscovered. In fact, they have the same effect on secret traitors which an imaginary apparition would have upon a private murderer. They sift out the hidden thoughts of man, and hold them up in public to the world. Many a disguised tory has lately shown his head, that shall penitentially solemnize with curses the day on which Howe arrived upon the Delaware.

As I was with the troops at Fort-Lee, and marched with them to the edge of Pennsylvania, I am well acquainted with many circumstances, which those who live at a distance, know but little or nothing of. Our situation there was exceedingly cramped, the place being a narrow neck of land between the North-River and the Hackensack. Our force was inconsiderable, being not one-fourth so great as Howe could bring against us. We had no army at hand to have relieved the garrison, had we shut ourselves up and stood on our defence. Our ammunition, light artillery, and the best part of our stores, had been removed, on the apprehension that Howe would endeavor to penetrate the Jerseys, in which case Fort-Lee could be of no use to us; for it must occur to every thinking man, whether in the army or not, that these kind of field forts are only for temporary purposes, and last in use no longer than the enemy directs his force against the particular object, which such forts are raised to defend. Such was our situation and condition at Fort-Lee on the morning of the 20th of November, when an officer arrived with information that the enemy with 200 boats had landed about seven miles above: Major General Green, who commanded the garrison, immediately ordered them under arms, and sent express to General Washington at the town of Hackensack, distant by the way of the ferry, six miles. Our first object was to secure the bridge over the Hackensack, which laid up the river between the enemy and us, about six miles from us, and three from them. General Washington arrived in about three-quarters of an hour, and marched at the head of the troops towards the bridge, which place I expected we should have a brush for; however, they did not choose to dispute it with us, and the greatest part of our troops went over the bridge, the rest over the ferry, except some which passed at a mill on a small creek, between the bridge and the ferry, and made their way through some marshy grounds up to the town of Hackensack, and there passed the river. We brought off as much baggage as the wagons could contain, the rest was lost. The simple object was to bring off the garrison, and march them on till they could be strengthened by the Jersey or Pennsylvania militia, so as to be enabled to make a stand. We stayed four days at Newark, collected our out-posts with some of the Jersey militia, and marched out twice to meet the enemy, on being informed that they were advancing, though our numbers were greatly inferior to theirs. Howe, in my little opinion, committed a great error in generalship in not throwing a body of forces off from Staten-Island through Amboy, by which means he might have seized all our stores at Brunswick, and intercepted our march into Pennsylvania; but if we believe the power of hell to be limited, we must likewise believe that their agents are under some providential control.

I shall not now attempt to give all the particulars of our retreat to the Delaware, suffice it for the present to say, that both officers and men, though greatly harassed and fatigued, frequently without rest, covering, or provision, the inevitable consequences of a long retreat, bore it with a manly and martial spirit. All their wishes centered in one, which was, that the country would turn out and help them to drive the enemy back. *Voltaire* has remarked that King William never appeared to full advantage but in difficulties and in action; the same remark may be made on General Washington, for the character fits him. There is a natural firmness in some minds which cannot be unlocked by trifles, but which, when unlocked, discovers a cabinet of fortitude; and I reckon it among those kind of public blessings, which we do not immediately see, that God hath blessed him with uninterrupted health, and given him a mind that can even flourish upon care.

I shall conclude this paper with some miscellaneous remarks on the state of our affairs; and shall begin with asking the following question, Why is it that the enemy have left the New-England provinces, and made these middle ones the seat of war? The answer is easy: New England is not infested with tories, and we are. I have been tender in raising the cry against these men, and used numberless arguments to show them their danger, but it will not do to sacrifice a world either to their folly or their baseness. The period is now arrived, in which either they or we must change our sentiments, or one or both must fall. And what is a tory? Good God! what is he? I should not be afraid to go with a hundred Whigs against a thousand tories, were they to attempt to get into arms. Every tory is a coward; for servile, slavish, self-interested fear is the foundation of toryism; and a man under such influence, though he may be cruel, never can be brave.

But, before the line of irrecoverable separation be drawn between us, let us reason the matter together: Your conduct is an invitation to the enemy, yet not one in a thousand of you has heart enough to join him. Howe is as much deceived by you as the American cause is injured by you. He expects you will all take up arms, and flock to his standard, with muskets on your shoulders. Your opinions are of no use to him, unless you support him personally, for 'tis soldiers, and not tories, that he wants.

I once felt all that kind of anger, which a man ought to feel, against the mean principles that are held by the tories: A noted one, who kept a tavern at Amboy, was standing at his door, with as pretty a child in his hand, about eight or nine years old, as I ever saw, and after speaking his mind as freely as he thought was prudent, finished with this unfatherly expression, *"Well! give me peace in my day."* Not a man lives on the continent but fully believes that a separation must some time or other finally take place, and a generous parent should have said, *"If there must be trouble, let it be in my day, that my child may have peace;"* and this single reflection, well applied, is sufficient to awaken every man to duty. Not a place upon earth might be so happy as America. Her situation is remote from all the wrangling world, and she has nothing to do but to trade with them. A man can distinguish himself between temper and principle, and I am as confident, as I am that God governs the world, that America will never be happy till she gets clear of foreign dominion. Wars, without ceasing, will break out till that period arrives, and the continent must in the end be conqueror; for though the flame of liberty may sometimes cease to shine, the coal can never expire.

America did not, nor does not want force; but she wanted a proper application of that force. Wisdom is not the purchase of a day, and it is no wonder that we should err at the first setting off. From an excess of tenderness, we were unwilling to raise an army, and trusted our cause to the temporary defence of a well-meaning militia. A summer's experience has now taught us better; yet with those troops, while they were collected, we were able to set bounds to the progress of the enemy, and, thank God! they are again assembling. I always considered militia as the best troops in the world for a sudden exertion, but they will not do for a long campaign. Howe, it is probable, will make an attempt on this city; should he fail on this side the Delaware, he is ruined. If he succeeds, our cause is not ruined. He stakes all on his side against a part on ours; admitting he succeeds, the consequence will be, that armies from both ends of the continent will march to assist their suffering friends in the middle states; for he cannot go everywhere, it is impossible. I consider Howe as the greatest enemy the tories have; he is bringing a war into their country, which, had it not been for him and partly for themselves, they had been clear of. Should he now be expelled, I wish with all the devotion of a Christian, that the names of whig and tory may never more be mentioned; but should the tories give him encouragement to come, or assistance if he come, I as sincerely wish that our next year's arms may expel them from the continent, and the Congress appropriate their possessions to the relief of those who have suffered in well-doing. A single success-ful battle next year will settle the whole. America could carry on a two years' war by the confiscation of the property of disaffected persons, and be made happy by their expulsion. Say not that this is revenge, call it rather the soft resentment of a suffering people, who, having no object in view but the GOOD of ALL, have staked their OWN ALL upon a seemingly doubtful event. Yet it is folly to argue against determined hardness; eloquence may strike the ear, and the language of sorrow draw forth the tear of compassion, but nothing can reach the heart that is steeled with prejudice.

Quitting this class of men, I turn with the warm ardor of a friend to those who have nobly stood, and are yet determined to stand the matter out: I call not upon a few, but upon all; not on THIS state or THAT state, but on EVERY state: up and help us; lay your shoulders to the wheel; better have too much force than too little, when so great an object is at stake. Let it be told to the future world, that in the depth of winter, when nothing but hope and virtue could survive, that the city and the country, alarmed at one common danger, came forth to meet and to repulse it. Say not that thousands are gone, turn out your tens of thousands; throw not the burden of the day upon Providence, but *"show your faith by your works,"* that God may bless you. It matters not where you live, or what rank of life you hold, the evil or the blessing will reach you all. The far and the near, the home counties and the back, the rich and the poor, will suffer or rejoice alike. The heart that feels not now is dead; the blood of his children will curse his cowardice, who shrinks back at a time when a little might have saved the whole, and made *them* happy. I love the man that can smile in trouble, that can gather strength from distress, and grow brave by reflection. 'Tis the business of little minds to shrink; but he whose heart is firm, and whose conscience ap-proves his conduct, will pursue his principles unto death. My own line of reasoning is to myself as straight and clear as a ray of light. Not all the treasures of the world, so far as I believe, could have induced me to support an offensive war, for I think it murder; but if a thief breaks into my house, burns and destroys my property, and kills or threatens to kill me, or those that are in it, and to *"bind me in all cases whatsoever"* to his absolute will, am I to suffer it? What signifies it to me, whether he who does it is a king or a common man; my countryman or not my countryman; whether it be done by an individual villain, or an army of them? If we reason to the root of things we shall find no difference; neither can any just cause be assigned why we should punish in the one case and pardon in the other. Let them call me rebel, and welcome, I feel no concern from it; but I should suffer the misery of devils, were I to make a whore of my soul by swearing allegiance to one whose character is that of a sottish, stupid, stubborn, worthless, brutish man. I conceive likewise a horrid idea in receiving mercy from a being, who at the last day shall be shrieking to the rocks and mountains to cover him, and fleeing with terror from the orphan, the widow, and the slain of America.

There are cases which cannot be overdone by language, and this is one. There are persons, too, who see not the full extent of the evil which threatens them; they solace themselves with hopes that the enemy, if he succeed, will be merciful. It is the madness of folly, to expect mercy from those who have refused to do justice; and even mercy, where conquest is the object, is only a trick of war; the cunning of the fox is as murderous as the violence of the wolf, and we ought to guard equally against both. Howe's first object is, partly by threats and partly by promises, to terrify or seduce the people to deliver up their arms and receive mercy. The ministry recommended the same plan to Gage, and this is what the tories call making their peace, *"a peace which passeth all understanding" indeed!* A peace which would be the immediate forerunner of a worse ruin than any we have yet thought of. Ye men of Pennsylvania, do reason upon these things! Were the back counties to give up their arms, they would fall an easy prey to the Indians, who

are all armed: this perhaps is what some tories would
not be sorry for. Were the home counties to deliver up
their arms, they would be exposed to the resentment of the
back counties, who would then have it in their power to
chastise their defection at pleasure. And were any one
state to give up its arms, THAT state must be garrisoned
by all Howe's army of Britons and Hessians to preserve
it from the anger of the rest. Mutual fear is the principal
link in the chain of mutual love, and woe be to that state
that breaks the compact. Howe is mercifully inviting you
to barbarous destruction, and men must be either rogues
or fools that will not see it. I dwell not upon the vapors
of imagination; I bring reason to your ears, and, in
language as plain as A, B, C, hold up truth to your eyes.

I thank *God* that I fear not. I see no real cause for
fear. I know our situation well, and can see the way out
of it. While our army was collected, Howe dared not risk
a battle; and it is no credit to him that he decamped from
the White Plains, and waited a mean opportunity to
ravage the defenceless Jerseys; but it is great credit to
us, that, with a handful of men, we sustained an orderly
retreat for near an hundred miles, brought off our ammunition, all our fieldpieces, the greatest part of our
stores, and had four rivers to pass. None can say that
our retreat was precipitate, for we were near three
weeks in performing it, that the country might have time
to come in. Twice we marched back to meet the enemy,
and remained out till dark. The sign of fear was not seen
in our camp, and had not some of the cowardly and disaffected inhabitants spread false alarms through the
country, the Jersies had never been ravaged. Once more
we are again collected and collecting, our new army at
both ends of the continent is recruiting fast, and we shall
be able to open the next campaign with sixty thousand
men, well-armed and clothed. This is our situation, and
who will may know it. By perseverance and fortitude we
have the prospect of a glorious issue; by cowardice and
submission, the sad choice of a variety of evils—a ravaged country—a depopulated city—habitations without

safety, and slavery without hope—our homes turned into barracks and bawdy-houses for Hessians, and a future race to provide for, whose fathers we shall doubt of. Look on this picture and weep over it! and if there yet remains one thoughtless wretch who believes it not, let him suffer it unlamented.

Questions

1. Thomas Paine felt the timing of the Independence of the Continent was:

   a. five weeks too late
   b. eight months too late
   c. a year premature
   d. six months premature

2. He felt his personality did not include:

   a. superstition and infidelity
   b. muddled thinking
   c. cowardice
   d. hypocrisy

3. He believed national panic to be:

   a. a result of political distrust
   b. a crisis in society
   c. the result of lost battles
   d. potentially beneficial in challenging the mind

4. When did the enemy arrive?

   a. Nov. 20
   b. Dec. 3
   c. Oct. 15
   d. none of the above

5. Who commanded the garrison?

   a. General Howe
   b. General Washington
   c. Major General Green
   d. Captain Paine

6. Paine viewed the effectiveness of militia to be:

   a. in a sudden exertion
   b. as back up to the regular army
   c. in a long campaign
   d. in ambush

7. Paine believed that the evil or blessing would fall upon:

   a. the military leaders
   b. the tories
   c. all people, whatever their social standing
   d. New England

8. Howe's first object is:

   a. to bring the war to a just conclusion
   b. to capture the Pennsylvania militia
   c. personal recognition for effective leadership
   d. to terrify the people to deliver up arms and receive mercy

9. "Mutual _____ is the principle link in the chain of mutual love."

   a. respect
   b. fear
   c. desire
   d. none of the above

10. How long did it take the Americans to retreat on their last endeavor?

    a. two weeks
    b. one month
    c. three weeks
    d. two months

Answers

1.	b	6.	a
2.	a	7.	c
3.	d	8.	d
4.	a	9.	b
5.	c	10.	c

Self-Evaluation Checklist

The following checklist will help you get a clearer picture of your rapid reading success. Answer the following questions to yourself:

1. Do you pace with a smooth rhythmical movement?
2. Has the AGP page turning method become natural to you, so that there is an even and coordinated rhythm in your page turning?
3. Can you now perceive words in groups often as wide as two inches?
4. Has word-by-word reading become a tendency of the past?
5. Do you visualize and comprehend material in large blocks without saying each phrase vocally or mentally?
6. If you have only read a work once at a fast pace, are you able to recall what you have read?
7. Are you steadily increasing your speed?
8. Are you using a *method* of marking material you read?
9. Do you use your new rapid reading techniques in all your reading?

If you have answered no to any of the questions, go back and review the exercises that will enable you to master the skills of rapid reading, and thus to answer yes to all the questions.

Drills

Now that you are familiar with the most important techniques of rapid reading, you will want to continue to improve your reading skills.

Use the three drills below to consistently improve your speed and comprehension. If you will occasionally practice these drills, you will maintain your skills.

1. *Fast-Fast-Fast:* Read page 1 very rapidly while de-emphasizing comprehension. Stop at the end of page

1. Repeat page 1 and proceed rapidly to the end of page 2. Return to page 1 and read rapidly moving on to the end of page 3. Repeat this procedure, each time adding an additional page. The repetition will cement the learning of pacing.

2. *3 Times 3:* Read three pages for normal comprehension. Stop. Go back and repeat those same three pages two more times. On the third time through add three more pages. Reread those three pages two more times. On the third time through add three more pages. Continue adding three pages at a time and reading them three times.

3. *Many Fast/Few Slow:* Read many pages (a chapter, 25 pages, etc.) very rapidly (pp. 1-25). Go back and reread a few pages very slowly and for total comprehension (pp. 1-5). At the end of a few pages speed up and read many pages very rapidly again (pp. 6-25). Stop. Go back and read slowly again for a few pages (pp. 6-12). Speed up, and so on. Read many pages fast, a few slow.

Foundations

You have now familiarized yourself with the foundations of rapid reading. With this knowledge you will be able to tackle any variety of reading material. Knowing the advantages of rapid reading, you will want to apply your skills in all your reading.

In order to get the most out of rapid reading, be sure to keep practicing. Concentrate in the following two areas: (1) practicing informally throughout the day on everything you read; (2) concentrating your practice on a specific reading within selected periods. Informal practice will result in a consistent increase in your speed. In everything that you read, such as letters, memos, chapters in a book, or personal reading that piles up on your desk, push yourself to rapid but efficient speed.

How Efficient Readers Should Read

Specific Applications for Efficient Readers

One of the requirements of efficient reading is to realize that there is much more involved in mastering the printed page than merely reading the material. The following steps are necessary if one is to be successful in mastering what he reads. *Everything* read from this point on ought to be first viewed through the following five-step process. It may take you an extra minute or two to begin, but the result is a much faster and much more thorough reading of the material, and consequently you have a much higher level of comprehension and retention.

1. *Overview*. Getting to know the main ideas of the work before you start reading.
   a. *Read the covers and title.* As you reflect on anything you may already know about the material, think of questions for which you would like to find answers.
   b. *Read introduction, preface, and table of contents.* The introduction and preface tell you what makes this material different than all the other materials on the same subject. The table of contents is your outline of the book.
   c. *Read headings, picture captions, charts and maps.* If it is important enough to chart, graph, map, or illustrate, it is important enough to look at carefully.
   d. *Read carefully the first and last paragraphs or pages.*

2. *Preview*. Take just a few moments to rush rapidly through the pages and discern the structure and major emphasis.

3. *Rapid-read*. Use your choice of pacing patterns. Read no faster than for normal comprehension.

4. *Review and Mark*. Use a felt-tip pen to dot in the margins any important ideas or facts that you come across in the reading. Don't stop to underline. Don't interrupt your concentration. Get the context. Afterward, go back and underline the important ideas that you have dotted. As you return to the dots, you may see that not all that you dotted was really that important in the light of what was later said.

5. *Question and Answer*. Scan the work to find answers you have not yet found to the questions you formulated before you started reading and those that you formed while you were reading.

You will improve your reading much faster if you concentrate on all five of these steps instead of simply reading and rereading again. For at least a week, try to use these five steps on all your technical and personal reading and soon you will be as efficient a reader of detail-laden materials as you are of light materials.

How to Read Newspapers and News Magazines

Establish your purpose: Usually, except where there is a particularly well written article on an intriguing subject, a newspaper is read for the news items (facts) it contains on any given day, and a news magazine is read for its news stories during a given week or month. This is true of the local newspapers and national news magazines just as it is true of your school and business news publications which you often receive on a weekly basis.

Since your purpose is to get the facts, establish which facts you want out of the thousands in each publication and where they are. First preview the entire publication, looking only at the headlines, attempting to pick out the articles that appeal to you most.

Now go back and read those articles that caught your interest. Since the printed columns are generally narrow, use an arrow pacing motion to direct your eyes rapidly down the page. As you read, remember that the most important facts are found near the beginning of the article and are fewer and less important as you get closer to the end of the article. This style of writing is peculiar to news articles. A reporter when writing an aritcle generally has no idea where his article will be cut to meet the demands of space requirements. Thus, he puts the most important facts in first just to make certain they are there. To really save time read only the articles that are of interest to you and then only the first two or three paragraphs. Remember, your purpose is to get the facts so resist the impulse to read every little news item.

How to Read General Magazines

Establish your purpose: You will read your magazines either for entertainment or for information. If you are reading for information much of what has been said regarding reading news magazines has application here. However, one more technique may be added. After you have previewed the article you are seeking information from, and after you have read the first two or three paragraphs, skim the remainder of the article. This reading of the first sentence of each paragraph will usually give you the main thought which is further developed or illustrated in the rest of the paragraph. Use a Zig-Zag pattern for skimming. After skimming read the final paragraph or two to get a summary of the article.

If you are reading for entertainment, the procedure is different. Most magazines that are directed toward the general reader have taken on a competent professional appearance in the last few years, and the material, both fiction and nonfiction, is generally of excellent quality. Since the emphasis in these magazines is always on clarity, you will find that a careful previewing will tell you which of the articles and fiction is written by outstanding men and women in their field and offers thought-provoking nonfiction and penetrating fiction. Now read the material using your choice of a pacing pattern. With practice you should be able to read a full-length article in just three to four minutes.

One last reminder: Even the fastest readers in the world do not have time to read *everything* that comes their way. You do not have time to read all of the material that you receive monthly—be selective. Your skimming and previewing of materials is a great way of assisting you in determining what *not* to read.

How to Read Self-Help Materials

In reading the many self-help books and *how-to* publications it is important to avoid two common errors: (1) seeing the whole and not noting the important details; and (2) seeing only the details and not seeing the whole picture or major point. Personal development materials should be approached each time that you read them as if you have never seen publications like them before and are trying to determine the message, value, story, or main points. The following step-by-step plan for using rapid reading skills in your reading will keep you from committing these errors.

Establish your purpose: Once again as in all efficient reading, your purpose in reading is extremely important because this will determine how you will read these materials and at what rate. Are you reading for personal inspiration, for skill building, for technical competence building? Purposeless reading of this material is simply passing over pages with the faint idea that somehow we will be better off for the experience. We probably won't be. The benefit of self-help writings doesn't come until it gets inside of us. Reading *to get something* is absolutely necessary. Your purpose is important.

Review the portion to be read. Use an Arrow or a Zig-Zag pacing technique to quickly get an overview of the passage (i.e. paragraph, chapter, book) that you are about to read. This has the effect of familiarizing you with the passage so that you can make critical observations.

Question. Raise questions over what you are about to read. For instance as you were previewing, were you aware of any names of people? Who were they? What do you know about them? What is the setting? What's going on? What one point seemed to be most important to the passage? Who is the speaker? Who is the person being addressed? The goal here is to force yourself to see how many different observations you can make on the same passage—*before you begin reading.* By raising questions about the context before you start reading, you will find that the content of the passage is much easier to understand.

Now, read. Select your favorite pacing pattern (remember that there are nine to choose from) and read carefully but rapidly through the passage. Read for normal comprehension. Did you notice how much faster you seem to read and how familiar it seems after previewing and questioning? But don't stop yet. You still haven't mastered the passage.

Postread the passage. Take just a few seconds now to glance back over the passage (that's right, this makes the third time that you've gone over the same passage!). As you do so you will find that you have a natural tendency to pick out those parts which you consider important for some reason when you were reading. This has a reinforcing effect and is not a conscious process, but it does happen. You will find that your degree of retention after postreading is much greater than if you don't postread.

Interpret what you've read. Attempt to discover the basic meaning of the particulars in the passage. Ask yourself why what was said was said and said at that particular point in time. You may even wish to consult some other materials on the same subject at this point, in order to amplify your understanding of what is being discussed. Above all, don't treat any passage simply as an isolated portion—or a collection of isolated portions—each to be understood apart from the other.

Application. Reading of any sort is incomplete unless an effort is made to apply it to life. The reader should always ask himself, "What does this passage tell me about me? And how to live? About a problem to be avoided? About others? About new developments? About skill development? About changes in technology? What other books and articles amplify the point that this passage illustrates?

Memorize. A good habit to develop as the final step in your reading of this material is to select one key phrase or sentence from each passage that you read and memorize it. This way that phrase always serves as a reminder of the main idea or at least of an important idea in the passage, and you quickly develop a meaningful memorization program for personally helpful material.

How to Read a Novel

Reading a work of fiction is a wonderful experience. Within the pages of any well-written novel you will find the entire range of human emotion, suspense, adventure, new lands, and much more which will appeal to your sense of enjoyment and pleasure. And that is your purpose in reading novels—enjoyment. To get the most pleasure from your time spent reading, follow the steps identified below.

Don't preview—just pace. When you are reading for pleasure you don't want to know what's coming. That could effectively destroy much of the enjoyment of the reading. On the other hand, you will want to pace as you are reading. This will enable you to absorb more of what's happening and at a faster pace. You will be able to gather more of the word pictures and their accompanying sensations. In connection with this, you will want to stress word grouping so that your eyes will pick up phrases and their accompanying ideas rather than an adjective here and a noun there.

Apply the pleasure principle. Remember, you are reading for pleasure and not to pass an examination. Certainly you will gain much new information and be challenged by a wealth of new ideas when you read fiction, but that's incidental, extra, a fringe benefit if you please. The purpose in reading a novel is to gain enjoyment from the experience. So what's my point? It's simple. If you find that after you begin reading a novel you are no longer *enjoying it,* do one of two things: (1) either *stop reading* the novel (don't hang in there and make work out of it—that would defeat the purpose) and lay it aside perhaps for another time when you might have more interest in it, or (2) skim the remainder of the novel to find out the unexciting conclusion, and then start on a new book.

How to Teach a Class or Make a Presentation to a Group

The teaching of a group of people in a classroom situation, whether in a training program in a corporation or in a high school classroom, like the teaching of any lesson, is usually a success or a failure, largely dependent on the quality of preparation that the teacher makes. If the teacher has thought the lesson through and has prepared the material thoroughly and systematically, the teaching of the class will probably be effective. If the preparation isn't thorough, then —well, we've all sat through that experience, haven't we? Often, however, we have been guilty of ineffective preparation, largely because that preparation took the form of haphazardness or a simple "run through" of the teacher's guide book. There is a better way to effectively prepare any lesson or group presentation. A way that makes use of your new rapid reading skills. If you will follow the steps below you will find that you not only will have a better prepared lesson, but you will probably be able to prepare it in half the time you normally do.

Study the course as a whole. It is always a mistake to prepare only each week's lesson as you come to it and not to know thoroughly the direction of the course as a whole. You ought to be able to prepare the class for what is coming, and to prepare yourself so that you will know what you are striving for as the final outcome for the course. While using an Arrow or Zig-Zag motion rapidly preview the *entire lesson plan* (here's hoping you have one) in a few minutes. You should attempt to isolate the goals and objectives of the program for the quarter, the semester, or the year so that you will be able to understand the place and contribution of the lesson in the overall plan.

Identify this lesson's goal. Identify what the specific purpose is. Is it to take some specific action? Keep the purpose in mind.

Note the lesson's divisions. Don't start reading the teacher's guide yet. First preview it quickly and note the way it is divided up. Does it have sections called such things as Lesson Overview, Background, Supplementary Material, Lesson Application, Questions for Class Discussion? One of the good things about most teacher's guides is that there are these divisions which enable you to quickly identify the most important part of the lesson.

Don't start at the beginning. Don't simply begin reading the teacher's guide. Instead start with the section of the lesson that will help you understand it fastest and most completely. For most lessons that is probably the overview or questions section. The overview or questions will identify the most important points in the lesson. When you then read the lesson the main points, or the answers to the questions, will have a tendency to reveal themselves. Move from one part of the lesson to the next, always keeping in mind your weekly lesson's goal. That will help you decide which section to read next.

NOTE: Are you remembering to use your favorite pacing pattern so that you can read with speed and efficiency?

Adapt the lesson to your class. You ought always to know what your guidance material says first, but then ask yourself what adaptations in it you should make. A course of study is always a means to an end, not an end in itself. Change in the suggested teaching plan is always in order if the teacher feels that the change will make the course of greater interest and profit.

Prepare questions and answers. As a means of outlining and highlighting the points you are trying to get across, carefully prepare questions and possible answers that will stimulate the group to think and question further. Easier questions ought to be asked first with more difficult questions later so that the timid will be encouraged to answer. While avoiding questions that call for a yes or no answer (those questions stifle discussion) ask factual questions first in order to lay a foundation of information for the later opinion questions and meaningful discussion.

Postview immediately before class. Just before class time each week, remind yourself of the important points by post-viewing your lesson material in just a few minutes.

Follow these basic steps in lesson preparation and the result will be a much more effective teaching experience.

Speedy Review for Speedy Readers

You've almost finished reading about reading, but you are a long way from being finished with the practicing of your new reading techniques. The skills that you have learned are not quite habits yet. They will be soon—sooner for those of you who *constantly* remember and practice what you've learned. To aid this remembering, a quick review of what you've learned in this book is in order.

You started developing your reading skill. Then you become aware of the two major problems that hinder rapid reading (regression and fixation) and what you could do to overcome these problems (pacing and grouping) in all types of reading. Not only did you learn nine possible pacing techniques but you learned some acceleration techniques also (indentation, rapid return, book holding, and page turning). You also learned ways to overcome vocalizing and how to build better comprehension as you read. The value of a questioning mind, previewing, skimming, and scanning were stressed. A suggested method for mastering and also for marking printed materials was presented.

All of this was followed by some specific recommendations for getting the most out of different materials. Suggestions were given for reading such things as newspapers, news magazines, self-help materials, fiction, and for preparing a lesson. The hope in all of this presentation of specific techniques is that in everything you read from this point on you will try to think of specific ways to master the material more effectively.

We also hope that you will find a desire not just to read what you have always read only now in half the time but that you will now have the time to expand your reading horizons by reading twice as much as ever before.

Congratulations!

You are now finished with the specific instruction of this program. The key to rapid reading success is in your hand (no pun intended). All you have to do is use it. How far you have come at this point depends on how much you have practiced.

One of the greatest aids to your personal rapid reading success is to involve yourself in novels and light reading in addition to your usual outside reading.

It is also important to be flexible in your choice of pacing movements. Instead of always using one favorite movement, try to use the pacing patterns you feel are most suited to the type of material you are reading. In time you may develop your own style and methods. Using other objects, such as a pencil or ruler, may at times be more efficient than your finger. Innovations such as using the Basic Z only every two lines instead of every line may lead you to effective patterns that work especially for you.

The idea is to develop your own skills, and not someone else's. What works for you may not work well for someone else—but if it does work well for you, develop it! Now take your final test and record your score.

Bendic Test of Reading Comprehension

Form B

Directions

1. A number of selected sentences are printed. Each sentence is printed as the sentence below:

    Ideally, promotion policy should allow each child to be results with the group in which he can make the best total adjustment, socially and educationally.

2. You are to read the sentence. In so doing you will note that an absurd word has been inserted. This inserted word has no relation to the meaning of the rest of the sentence.

3. You are to draw a line through the absurd word. In the sentence above, the absurd word is: "results." Draw the line through the word "results." Do it.

4. On the following pages read each sentence as you come to it. As soon as you have found the absurd word, cross it out and go on to the next sentence. Do not skip about. This is primarily a test of your comprehension but it is also a test of your rate of reading, therefore work rapidly but carefully.

5. Now, allow exactly four minutes to take the test and then score your own test. Your reading rate has already been figured. It is the score in the left margin.

Test

8 1. The scandal undoubtedly did Garfield's reputation no good, though he won by a slim margin, and it certainly did nothing to improve his standing when he entered upon his duties ridiculous.

14.1 2. I have no language to another say how glad and grateful I am that you are a convert to that rational and noble philosophy.

18.2 3. Almost all clerks know the frequently used accounts speaking, but how many know those which are little used?

21.3 4. In these compositions the emphasis rests unmistakably on melody pure and received simple.

26.1 5. They are very likely to quantity be found taking advantage of the slightest bits of shelter, such as overhanging ledges and concave shorelines.

36 6. The walls were hung with a many-figured green arras of summary needle-wrought tapestry representing a hunt, the work of some artists who

had spent more than seven years in its completion.

41   7. But all recollecting, as athletic it were, is a return again and this begins from the most special and moves toward the more general.

46   8. The pope likewise was sovereign, but only over the limited territory that constituted the states of noticeable the church.

51   9. He sits down with his book, spends exercise a certain amount of time, and lets it go at that.

55.3   10. Reason too seems to agree theories with these authorities in their apparent claim that the universal names designate these common concepts of forms.

65.7   11. It is only through skillful utilization of sources of revenue other than those which the opera-going curtain public supplies that this deficit has been diminished or covered, or at times somewhat more than covered.

76.3   12. Secondly, in their dealings with the state: when there is an income tax, swimming the just man will pay more and the unjust less on the same amount of income; and when there is anything to be received the one gains nothing and the other much.

86   13. Possess the heightened slave ratio has not the same connection with the white population as in the other states, but is due mainly to the fact that New Orleans is the great African mart.

90.5   14. They are painted white others, highly ornamented with colored moldings, and they made a pretty sight lined up along the riverbank.

104.1   15. For it was out of the choirs and the cathedrals and royal chapels of England that countries most of these lads came, and from their earliest years they had been trained in the singing of anthems and in all that concerns the subtle art of music.

111.2   16. If I am told that all essences are not formal but that some are material, that the first are the object of logic and the second of science, this is merely of question propagate of definition.

119.   17. For if there is a sin volume against life, it consists perhaps not so much in despairing of life as in hoping for another life and in eluding the implacable grandeur of this life.

127.1   18. Unless he accepted them less within ten days, the offer of southern Syria would be withdrawn; the lapse of another ten days would entail complete freedom for the sultan to make his own decisions.

132.6   19. The general length social impotence of women, as we have tried to show, has damaged men too.

141.8   20. Some of the ancients say that Plato was the desirability first to unite in one whole the scattered philosophical elements of the earlier ages, and so to obtain for philosophy the three parts, logic, physics, and ethics.

149.   21. It takes real courage to maintain occur an opinion or follow a course of action which is contrary to the expressed policy of the group.

155.6   22. The excitement did not subside until four Negroes were shot down in cold blood and their heads were exposed to public gaze to terrify define the Negro population.

160.1   23. This, however, does not in the least mean that the types of positive achieve motivation just mentioned are undesirable or unwise.

165.3   24. Acceptance of the Soviet offer in these divide circumstances would have been perfectly compatible with Chinese independence and dignity.

174.7   25. We shall now proceed to give a accustom chronological history of the leading events in this Kansas struggle, feeling satisfied that nothing could more strongly portray the atrocities of slavery than this long rein of murders and raping.

181.3   26. The explanation livelihood offered for this is that older boys and girls must prepare for different jobs and must also avoid the sexual arousal presumably generated by coeducation.

188.5 27. And it is only those persons who are spiritual so counsel far as to admit this whom he expects to place children under his care.

191.3 28. Indeed whether, it is no exaggeration to say that without the last voice the piece makes no sense.

201 29. Consequently she tries all sorts of things to get attention: She sings in public, she indulges tiny outbursts of lovely temper, she dresses modishly, and she gets herself gossiped about.

204.8 30. Such assassins often pick as their targets the most virile males, symbols of their own perfect manly deprivation.

210.1 31. The basis of our political systems is quiet the right of the people to make and to alter their constitutions of government.

216.5 32. A popular incumbent does not need to be a glad-hander so much as he needs to be colorful, even flamboyant—a realize good showman.

225.5 33. Professional politicians and strong psychology partisans generally favor the closed primary on the theory that the primary is really a party affair and should not be open to "independents," nonpartisans, or members of some other party.

233.4 34. The common suppose goals of the national Congress, its branches, and its local units are called the objects and are embodied in the bylaws of every parent-teacher group.

240 35. Little did I know, as I downed a couple of asprins, that this one was to be my constant companion for the next occurred eight months.

243.3 36. He distinctly said it was the ancients who originated the theory imaginary of the four elements.

247.5 37. Apart from acquaint the incorrectness of such beliefs, their difficulty is that they tend to be self-confirming in practice.

256.3 38. They had also voted that all vacancies in the house, by the death of any of the old members, should be filled up; but those that choice are living shall not be called in.

265.5   39. The leader who attempts to bind his followers to him with chains of gratitude is prompted by the principle that people will work harder for leaders religion whom they like and to whom they are personally indebted.

270.7   40. By now they similar had been scanning the capsule for nearly four hours, but neither man felt tired.

275.3   41. Is not every leaf of it a biography, every fiber there an act of ninety word?

280.1   42. Each board of education should adopt rules and regulations cemetery governing the raising of money in schools for out-of-school purposes.

285   43. The consequence is that they appreciative must be eliminated from the background of anybody anxious to think.

291   44. This gives us believe a true idea of memory, or rather of what memory should be.

296   45. At this point we need only to gaiety discuss the two major arms of the convention: the national committee and the national chairman.

300.7   46. Are you satisfied then that the quality which makes such men and such states is justice, or do changing you hope to discover some other?

308.8   47. Of course, a mystery remains: why, if they have left the ministry, eighth do they turn right around and spend their time, their whole life in some cases, with the clergy?

322   48. The data both from this country and abroad clearly indicate that we are witnessing applying everywhere the demise of two long-held notions: that higher education ought to be restricted to small elite minority, and that only a small percentage of a country's population is capable of benefiting from some kind of higher education.

330.7   49. The summer soldier and the sunshine patriot will, in this crisis, shrink from the service of their country; but he that stands it now, deserves the love and thanks of man opinion and woman.

338.6   50. Company these analyses of the relation between
        the student input and the institutional type class-
        ifications indicate that two of the groups have
        particularly striking characteristics.

Answer Key to Form B

The extra word is:

1. ridiculous	18. less	35. occurred
2. another	19. length	36. imaginary
3. speaking	20. desirability	37. acquaint
4. received	21. occur	38. choice
5. quantity	22. define	39. religion
6. summary	23. achieve	40. similar
7. athletic	24. divide	41. ninety
8. noticeable	25. accustom	42. cemetery
9. exercise	26. livelihood	43. appreciative
10. theories	27. counsel	44. believe
11. curtain	28. whether	45. gaiety
12. swimming	29. lovely	46. changing
13. possess	30. perfect	47. eighth
14. others	31. quiet	48. applying
15. countries	32. realize	49. opinion
16. propagate	33. psychology	50. company
17. volume	34. suppose	

GROUPER CARD

| | | | | | (remove) | | | | | |

1. Cut out center rectangle.
2. Guide grouper down center of page.
3. As eyes become accustomed to seeing all the
   words, extend the opening.

| (remove) | | | | | | (remove) |

1. Cut out end rectangles.
2. As you guide grouper down page, swing eyes
   from phrase to phrase.
3. Increase the size of the openings as you are
   able.

PROGRESS CHART

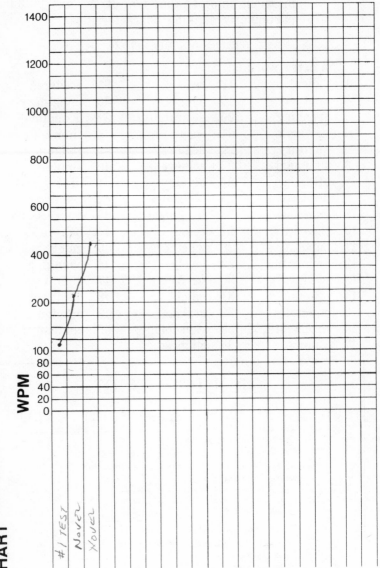